725

The Changing Church

NG CHURCH

Its Architecture, Art, and

Decoration

by

Katharine Morrison McClinton

Morehouse-Gorham Co.

New York

1957

PRINTED IN THE UNITED STATES OF AMERICA

BY SOWERS PRINTING COMPANY, LEBANON, PA.

To

Catharine Rule Ashley

and

Chase Whitcher Ashley

THE ILLUSTRATION USED ON THE TITLE PAGE

The severe design of Zion Lutheran Church, Portland, Oregon, is balanced by a warmth of expression in the choice and handling of materials. There are no painted or stained surfaces. Narrow redwood battens, spaced on Sitka spruce, form a reredos of simple beauty, against which gleams the large copper cross. The altar is of embossed copper, with the church seal in the front center. The candelabra are brass.

The lining of the apertures in the brick wall are copper. The chancel screen windows are of orchid and amber glass, and the windowless nave is lighted from spotlights in the ceiling. Green asphalt tile covers the floor, with green carpet in the chancel.

Pietro Belluschi, architect.

6

Foreword

*I*T is a pleasant honor to be asked to write an introduction to a book that promises to be of use in the design of church architecture and the allied arts.

The wealth of material that Katharine Morrison McClinton here presents has long been needed. The text is in language that should be a pleasure for the working member of a building committee to read; and the illustrations have been selected to include solutions for alterations and improvements of older ecclesiastical buildings as well as fine solutions of contemporary architecture.

Real consideration on the part of those proposing to build should be given to the author's pleas for the careful programming of all the various devotional, educational, and social requirements of a congregation in relation to its community, for the purchase of sufficient property for the buildings together with outdoor recreational facilities and off-street parking of motor cars, and for a preliminary master plan to envisage future expansion of the group of buildings, even though only a portion of the group is proposed for immediate construction.

There is one other plea of which I, as a professional man, am most appreciative. Mrs. McClinton calls for a fluid approach to the problems of architectural design and urges the delegating of such problems to the architect for his solution.

But even more important than these outlines for planning and building procedures is the author's sensitivity to the fact that we live, build, and embellish our churches in the second half of the twentieth century; and that the responsibility of the Church in rendering ever increasing services in a changing society has made it inadvisable for any congregation to burden itself in an attempt to construct costly imitations of the buildings of an earlier era.

One nineteenth-century writer, in a dangerously sentimental approach to scholarship in the fine arts, once referred to a work of architecture as "frozen music." This it is not. But it may be said that any given structure is the frozen economics, sociology, and even anthropology of the times in which it is erected.

But architecture is much more than this. It is the useful and poetically beautiful expression in monumental abstract sculpture of the delight existing in any era between man and his environment.

FREDERICK DUNN, A. I. A.

December 15, 1956

Preface

*T*HERE is little information on how to build a beautiful church in the terms of today's living. Yet the Church speaks in buildings as well as sermons. This book is written to assist the clergy and members of building committees and architects in solving some of the practical problems of building a new church or remodeling an old one. It is written to help you whatever your church decorating problem, be it only the selecting of new cushions for the pews.

The book is also written with the express purpose of improving the taste and creating a demand for better design in the building and decorating of present-day churches.

I wish to thank the many contemporary architects whose churches are illustrated in this book and whose work more than any other factor influenced the writing of it. Among the architects who gave of their time as well as photographs of their work are Charles Woodbridge, Edward Coe Embury, and Maurice R. Salo. I am particularly indebted to Frederick Dunn, who is a member of the Episcopal Church Joint Commission on Church Architecture and the Allied Arts and of the Commission on Architecture, Department of Worship and the Arts, of the National Council of Churches, for reading the manuscript and making suggestions, and for writing the Foreword. For reading and suggestions on a part of the manuscript, I wish to thank the Rev. William A. Blondon, rector of St. Paul's-in-the-Desert, Palm Springs, California, and Mr. Lewis Smith, lighting consultant, for suggestions on the chapter on Church Lighting. For notes on church carpets, I owe my thanks to Mr. Carl J. Olsen of W & J Sloane & Co., and for valuable information from his decorating experience, Mr. Viggo Rambusch. I also wish to thank the artists and sculptors and the National Sculpture Society and each church illustrated for permission to use the photographs. Especial thanks are due to Charles Nagel of the City Art Museum of St. Louis for his suggestions and advice on the selection of illustrations.

A note of thanks to my husband, Harold D. McClinton, for suggesting the title of the book.

For the information on present-day needlework projects, I wish to thank Mrs. William W. Hoppin, Mrs. Eugene W. Stetson, Mrs. Stephen F. Bayne, Mrs. Bernard C. Newman, and the various chairmen and designers of the projects at Trinity Church, New York City, and the National Cathedral, Washington, D. C.

KATHARINE MORRISON McCLINTON

New York City
August, 1956

Contents

Detail from stained glass by Emil Frei, Faith-Salem Evangelical and Reformed Church, Jennings, Missouri. Frederick Dunn, architect. (See also pages 130 and 131.)

1

Church Architecture and Decoration: The New Point of View

MORE churches are being built or rebuilt in America today than ever before. The building and renovation movement is universal, and approximately ninety per cent of the churches in the country have recently been engaged in some kind of building program. Large cities are building cathedrals, small cities and country congregations are building churches of smaller size and simpler design. Chapels are being built at airports, on ocean liners, at colleges, and in National Parks, such as the Chapel of the Ages in the Grand Canyon. What are these new churches like? It is hard to believe, but statistics show that one in every four is of modern design rather than traditional period style. But whether traditional or modern, church architecture is changing. Indeed it is changing more rapidly than the average architect realizes, and certainly much faster than the thinking of most church building committees.

The great building program of the American churches puts a tremendous responsibility upon those of the clergy and congregations taking part in the building and decorating of a new church. Indeed, unless guide lines are made for the clergy, architects, and people we will have new churches with no more taste and inspiration than the old ones that we are replacing. Many unattractive and inadequate churches have been built and are still being built. First, because church committees are not sure of what they want, and, second, architects are not conversant with the church needs. The average committee member is a successful business man and he is concerned with the efficient equipment of the building. He uses his knowledge of constructing a school, a fac-

tory, or an office building in advising about the church building. He wants an efficient building, a good auditorium with acoustical qualities and comfortable seats. One building committee that I know of spent months literally sitting in church pews of various designs and trying them out to see if they were comfortable. Then, too, church committees are made up of members who still want churches with a "dim religious light," and to whom the only answer in church decoration is a modified form of Gothic architecture.

There are also architects who, even though they have built many churches, do not know the needs of the particular church—mainly because the building committee has not made them clear. Then there are architects who are still translating architectural styles of other ages. And there are modern architects who are following the cliché of placing an off center cross, or bringing in the out-of-doors by means of conservatory windows or window boxes which remind one of the non-sectarian churches at Forest Lawn. Also there is the architect who has too often conformed to the building committee's ideas rather than turn down a lucrative commission. To build a successful church, the architect must be the sole creator of the design. Once the design is created the building committee can extend it, but the architect must handle and control the building committee, and have the final "say."

After all, the architect is engaged for his expert advice and it is foolish to lose money by ignoring his ideas. The whole situation can be cleared up by education on both sides and by the architect managing the project architecturally and the committee spending its time making a survey of the

San Lorenzo Community Church, Congregational, San Lorenzo, California. Formerly the famous Navy "Seabee" chapel of Camp Parks. Parabolic form in brick, glass, and plastic, accented by the white cross of contemporary form. The planting harmonizes with the lines of the architecture. Bruce Goff, architect.

church needs. A building is a work of art and as such must be a personal expression of the artist, and not of a committee. Yet the committee and not the architect must take the blame for such practical mistakes as were made when recently enlarging a small Western church. The seating capacity of the nave was doubled, a lavatory was added to the clergy's sacristy, but there were no closets for the clergy's vestments.

Too often the building committee decide on Gothic or New England Colonial architecture because they have no basis to judge any other type and they feel safe in choosing what is familiar. The style of architecture should be considered after the requirements of the interior have been met by the inside plan. In other words, the plan must be perfected and then the form of the exterior grows out of the plan and establishes itself.

It is hard to advise laymen how to judge either historic or modern architecture. The best way is to educate them first in the historical styles of architecture and in the meaning of each style. A lecture course with slides of the various styles of church architecture—Greek, Roman, Byzantine, Romanesque, Gothic, and Renaissance, showing both antique and adapted versions of each style —would provide a good background. Visits to churches of different types and notes on the most impressive building visited would also prove helpful. But more important still would be a course in the appreciation of good design, which is the basis of all good architecture whatever its style. For style is only the surface expression. The materials that the architect really works with are form, proportion, balance, scale, texture, color, and light and shade. A good architect can handle these elements of design so that a building will be beautiful, even if it is constructed of concrete and redwood instead of marble and stone. Good design is a matter of creative imagination, not of materials.

But building any successful building means not only constructing a beautiful structure, but one that meets the needs of its occupants and is in tune with the times in which it is built. Architecture does more than merely utilize natural forms

—arches, pillars, rectangles, cylinders, and spheres. It expresses their characteristic effect upon the observer. Thus a building is called a castle, a palace, a theater, or a church.

A church must first of all meet the purpose for which it is designed. A church is built for worship. To be satisfactory, the church building must express this purpose. A house must also express the character and taste of its owner. The church is God's House and as such it must have a feeling of God. It must have beauty, spirituality, and dignity. It must not only be beautiful to look at, but it must make men want to remain to pray. It is not enough that the seats are comfortable and that the music is excellent, and the decorations cheerful. A church ought to have peace and repose. It should inspire and preserve man's feeling of the ultimate beyond time and space. Thus the building should draw people by its atmosphere of harmony, peace, and dignity. Architecture accomplishes this by its purity of form, simple straightforwardness, and by a subordina-

tion of every detail to the principal lines of the design. In a church this is most easily accomplished by a return to the liturgical arrangement of an altar, or communion table, in the sanctuary at the eastern end of the church. Many non-liturgical churches, such as the Presbyterian and the Methodist, have now adopted this plan instead of that with the pulpit in the center. With the altar as a dominant central focal point, it is easier to tie all the other elements of the design into a unified whole.

A church should also express awe and wonder. It should stir the imagination. Religion is partly an emotional experience and a church needs to stir the emotions. Architecture, alone, can be made emotional, but it is aided by beauty of color, by music, and even by good oratory.

The church also needs brilliance and drama. This can be accomplished by the use of light, murals, mosaics, and symbolic designs, or it may be done by means of dramatic proportion, with an emphasis or exaggeration of line. The Church of

Robert F. Carr Memorial Chapel of St. Savior, Illinois Institute of Technology. Constructed of brick, steel, and glass. The altar is of unadorned Roman Travertine marble. The cross and simple altar rail are of stainless steel. Behind the altar hangs a silk curtain. Mies van der Rohe, architect.

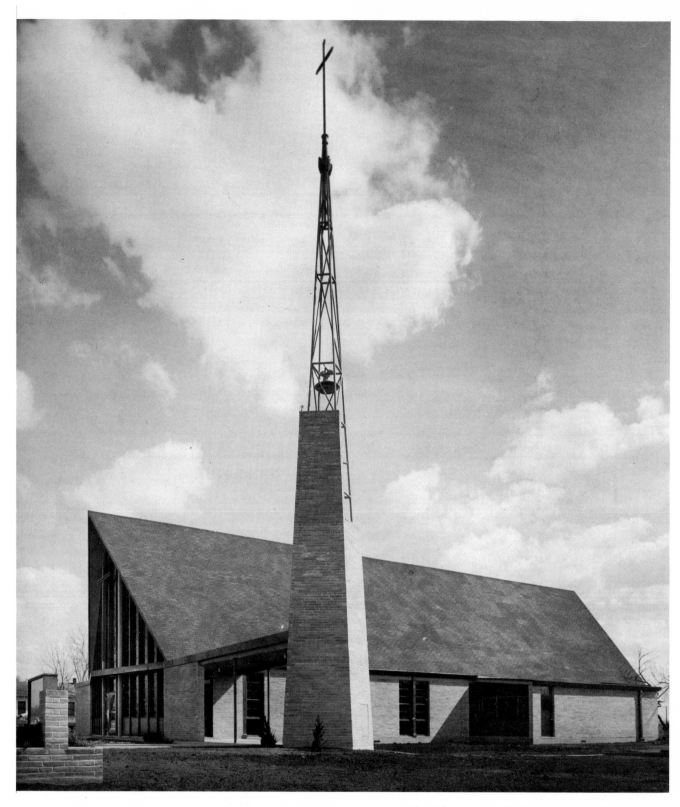

Concordia Lutheran Church, San Antonio, Texas. Exterior walls of Mexican handmade brick (Norman size), exposed brick on interior. Entire front wall and nave windows at wood arches are of gray-green Blenko glass. Clear glass in sanctuary windows provides view of planting areas from Communion rail. Spire of pipe frame, with brick base. Henry Steinbomer, architect.

the Epiphany, New York City, gains brilliance through simplicity of materials and forms and an accent and exaggeration of the vertical line. The architectural style is an adaptation of Gothic, though one is not conscious of any style, but only of the spiritual uplift of the design.

A church should also be Spartan in atmosphere, giving an appearance of strength and courage, for religion is never soft and easy. It should be sincere, simple, and restrained, but have the warmth of welcome. An inviting entrance of good-sized proportions, a colorful door, or a properly placed window extends a welcome. If a door is too small or unattractive, it may be enhanced by attractive planting of trees or shrubs or by painting it a pleasing color.

As a House of God, a church has certain specific requirements for worship. First of all there is the sanctuary, where the altar is placed and where the worship is centered. It is a mistake to economize on the size of the chancel, of the sanctuary, or of the altar, for here is the focal point of worship. The modern church-in-the-round places the altar in the center which gives a sense of fellowship and togetherness.

The lectern and pulpit are also a necessary part of the mechanics of worship. These should not only be placed where the congregation can see and hear, but they should be attractive in design, well lighted, and of proper size and proportions in relation to the other elements of the chancel. In a small church, the lectern can be omitted and the lessons read from the altar.

The choir and the organ are also necessary parts of church worship and should be carefully considered in the architectural plan of the church. The organ as a center of interest and decoration is no longer used. Indeed if there is any church which needs remodeling, it is the one built on the old plan of organ pipes with choir above and behind the pulpit. This choir was built for a quartet of singers and is now outmoded. The modern trend is for larger choirs and bigger music budgets. Even non-liturgical congregations have become dissatisfied with organ pipes as the dominant point of interest in their churches.

When considering these necessary and concrete factors of worship, the architect and the building committee should never lose sight of the need to establish and preserve an atmosphere of worship. This can be done by the creation of significant architectural form, by the use of line, tone, color, and even by the psychological use of artificial lighting.

Another factor in church design is the congregation. The church is no longer a place for idle contemplation. The congregation today comes together to worship and to work. People follow the church service with prayer book and hymnal, or at least by the use of the printed program. Therefore good light for reading is necessary. The changes in church lighting, as well as the decorative and psychological aspects of light, will be taken up in the chapter on lighting.

The church congregation today also wants to hear. Not only do they want to hear the sermon and the music, but they want to hear and to follow the service. This means that the church must have good acoustics. Indeed, today's acoustical requirements shape the architectural plan. The design of a church should never be completed without the aid of an acoustical consultant. He may suggest a slight slant of a wall which will keep out sound flutter or the use of materials that aid acoustics. His fee will cost less than microphones and be more satisfactory.

The city church also needs to have noise and dirt shut out. This is being done by installing cooling fans and air conditioning. Churches built without windows are another means of shutting out noise. The Church of St. Clement, in Alexandria, Virginia, is an effective example of a modern church without windows. There are pinpoint lights in the ceiling and spotlights to pick up the focal points such as the altar and pulpit.

The present-day congregation also demand a certain degree of comfort in their worship. They need the comfort of heat in winter. They need a church free from draughts. The church whose back pews are flooded with draughts of cold from the outside whenever the door opens for a late-comer can no longer hope to keep these pews filled. A glass partition between the nave and vestibule or narthex will solve this problem without interfering with the architectural design. More and more churches are finding that air con-

Faith-Salem Evangelical and Reformed Church, Jennings, Missouri. The brick work is salmon pink "Chicago Commons." Wall of glass by Emil Frei. Frederick Dunn & Associates, architects. (See also pages 130 and 131.)

Church of St. Clement, Episcopal, Alexandria, Virginia. Simple architectural mass with cross and mural by Robert Davidson. Joseph Saunders, Jr., architect.

ditioning is paid for by the increase in summer congregations. Perhaps the South is more advanced than any other part of the country in this matter. However, St. Bartholomew's Church in New York City is now air conditioned, which adds to the comfort of summer weddings and funerals as well as the regular Sunday and weekday services. Churches in the desert at Palm Springs, California, have air cooling systems which make them comfortably cool although the outside temperature is over one hundred degrees.

Comfortable seats are also an aid to good worship, but they should not be so comfortable that they make for napping. Consideration should be taken as to their correct height, the width of the seat, and the spacing between pews. The size and height of kneeling pads are also important.

The present-day extended activities of the church include not only worship, but work. They include teaching, fellowship, and service. The church buildings are no longer just a place for Sunday service and Sunday school, for church activities have extended so that the buildings are used throughout the week. The extended activities of the Sunday school include music, drama, and pageantry. Church luncheons, suppers, dances for the young people, basketball courts, and even swimming pools provide fellowship.

More and more couples are being married in the church, and in spite of the "Funeral Churches," more and more people are asking for funeral services in their own church, and more children than ever before are being baptized. All these services make demands on the space requirements of the present-day church. With these extended activities there is often an overlapping of services and this requires more and better means of getting in and out. There must also, even in the small church, be provision for the larger congregations at Christmas and Easter. Some churches settle this problem by having the service piped into an extra chapel or auditorium, or by having two identical services. A new church building can provide for these enlarged seasonal congregations by the use of sliding doors or folding partitions between church and chapel or Sunday school rooms.

Extended activities of the church also require more parking space for cars and a larger site for the church building. Large grounds in turn require a landscaping plan. In climates that can make use of the church grounds, gardens can be used not only as a setting for the church, but to supply flowers for the church, and as a place for meetings of committees and small groups.

Along with the changes in the activities of churches there are the changes in the building world that also affect the design and construction

Macdolen Chapel, Fort Wayne, Indiana. The twelve-foot figure of Christ is executed in Indiana limestone. The stately dignity of the figure harmonizes with the stone architecture of the building. Eugene Kormendy, sculptor.

of the church. Building costs have been increased. Mass production has brought in mechanical equipment and new building materials in metals, minerals, and plastic glass. In order to construct a church that is not prohibitive in price, the present-day architect is not only forced to simplify his design, but to use these new materials. The acceptance of these contemporary materials has brought about a new contemporary design, and instead of the adaptation of old styles of architecture the architects have unlimited variations of form. It is left to the resourcefulness of the modern architect to build with beauty and dignity within these expanded horizons. He must, to a certain extent, build with line and proportion instead of ornament, for a maximum of architectural expression at low cost. The emphasis must be on structural lines rather than decoration. This more simplified church architecture must make use of structural glass, steel, aluminum, and wood in such a way that they become decoration. The effects of this architecture are dependent upon the directness of its use of these natural raw materials which will bring out the underlying spiritual power of pure form and the dignity of simple materials simply used. The living church must build in the spirit of the age and in a contemporary architecture. The Gothic, Renaissance, and Georgian churches were all contemporary architecture that spoke the language of their time.

The trend toward contemporary church architecture is influenced by building costs. A free-form building is much less expensive to construct than a building of the same square footage in traditional Gothic or Georgian. And the trend toward the wooden church of laminated construction is also influenced by cost.

However, we should not lose sight of the fact that on the long range basis of cost, stone is an economical building material for churches. When stone is used there is no need for costly painting. Stone needs no protection against decay or termites, and it will not peel off from exposure to weather. Stone is the material of permanence. The beauty of stone allows for an infinite variety of texture, color, and sculptural detail. Stone is found in a great variety of color and texture. Thus a church may be built entirely of one kind of stone or it may use several different kinds for contrasts, such as Indiana limestone for walls, Travertine or flagstone on floors, and marble for the altar.

Architect's model of First Evangelical Church, Santa Ana, California. Frederick Hodgdon, architect.

2

The Elements of Design as Related to Church Architecture and Decoration

THIS chapter is for the clergy and building committee. The principles set forth are familiar to all architects; indeed they are the tools of his trade. However, factors of design have to be considered even in the smallest replacement jobs in church decoration. If no architect or trained decorator is at hand, it is well for the building committee to have more than their personal likes or dislikes for guidance. Even a small item like the placing of a memorial plaque can mar the appearance of a church wall. Altar candlesticks which are too large or too small for the altar can detract from the service, and even the color of the pew cushions can be either offensive or harmonious with the rest of the church decorations. Thus the smallest detail needs careful consideration so that it will not only be suitable for its purpose but harmonious with the church as a whole. Even one endowed with ordinary good taste needs extra knowledge of design and color in relation to architecture and the special needs of church architecture. Designing a church is far different from building a house or an office building, and the best architect in the world cannot design a church unless he has had special training in ecclesiastical design.

Architecture, along with sculpture and painting, is a space art. In the space arts there are three structural elements with which harmonious designs may be built up. These are line, form, and color. These three factors must be considered whether you are designing a church or merely placing a piece of memorial sculpture.

Space is the chief element in architecture. Lines are boundaries that define spaces and interrelations of lines and spaces. Nature does not present us with lines in isolation. Lines are of different types with different expressions and meanings. The upright or vertical line, the dominant line in Gothic architecture, is aspiring and uplifting. The vertical line is also emotional and mystical. The horizontal line is earthbound and more intellectual. A church that is broad in relation to its height (the fault of most late nineteenth-century Protestant churches) presents a matter-of-fact view of life and religion. Curved lines are soft and graceful. A wavering line is indecisive, and a zigzag line is harsh and repellent and expresses too much movement.

The simplest piece of well-designed furniture and the greatest cathedrals have in common good line design as the structure on which all other elements of their beauty are built. If you can look at two chests of drawers or two arrangements of line in a square or rectangle and choose the better of the two, you have exercised your ability to appreciate good design and can put that ability to work to judge the better of two architectural drawings for a church.

Spacing is the groundwork of design; the success of any design depends on just how lines are arranged within a space. There are certain ways of spacing which are rules of composition. These apply equally to the painting of a picture, the modeling of a piece of sculpture, or to the designing of a church. These rules are:

1. Opposition
2. Transition
3. Subordination
4. Repetition
5. Symmetry

Claremont Community Church, Claremont, California. Good architectural proportions form setting for artistic detail. Altar mosaic by Jean and Arthur Ames. Theodore Criley, architect.

Two lines meeting form a simple and severe harmony called opposition. Examples of opposition are found in a simple plaid design, a Greek doorway, and a plain unadorned cross. The effect of opposition of straight lines is severe and abrupt. For this reason the straight line is often softened by transition. In architecture, the capital forms a transition between the column and the architrave. The pediment softens the appearance of the doorway, and the slanting roof makes a transition between the rectangle of the church and the steeple as seen in a typical New England church design. Thus transition harmonizes the abrupt difference of line into unity.

The element of subordination is of utmost importance in design, especially church design. This means that one factor or part is dominant and all other parts must be subordinate. In a church exterior, the steeple or tower, if there is one, should be dominant and all other parts of the building should be subordinate to it. In the church interior, the chancel should be the dominant part of the plan and all other parts should be subordinate, but related, to it. Subordination may be accomplished by making one object dominant in size, or it may be done by grouping objects so that they give prominence or attention to the object of first importance. An object may also be made dominant by means of color or by contrast of light and dark tone. Thus a small altar of dark stone will look larger and more dominant against a light or medium tone wall than against a dark wall where it is lost from sight. A small window with bright colored glass will look more important than the same window with plain panes of neutral tones. Thus many churches built with plain glass windows with the hope of replacing these with decorative memorial windows find that the brilliant windows when in place may detract from the chancel itself. Of course, when all details of color and design are carefully planned and executed as planned, although many years later, this does not happen.

Repetition produces beauty by repeating the same lines or forms. Pillars of churches and colonnades of arches create architectural repetition. A border of meanders or scrolls produces repetition. To be successful, the repetition must be rhythmical, not a mere row of repeated objects. We have rhythmical repetition in nature with night and day, or the seasons, which recall, but never quite repeat, themselves. Fences and railroad tracks built with mathematical repeats are examples of uninteresting rhythm. An oriental rug with its center and border all repeating the same motifs and lines, yet in different sizes and

Interior of St. Paul's Chapel of Trinity Parish, New York City. The oldest public building on Manhattan Island and one of the most beautiful examples of Georgian architecture still in existence in its original form.

St. Mark's Episcopal Church, St. Louis, Missouri. The white brick walls are painted gray. The aisles are dark red, vermilion, and black tile. The altar is violet-veined white marble with trim of purple slate and gold mosaic. The cross is of pewter, brass, and red leather and has a baldachin of off-white wood polychromed in blue, gold, silver, vermilion, and violet. Nagel and Dunn, architects.

relationships, is an example of good rhythm and harmonious design.

Symmetry is the simplest way to create order and balance. Two objects are put in exact balance as on a teeter board. The placing of a window on either side of a door gives symmetrical balance. The two sides of a vase are symmetrical. The two rows of Gothic arches in a cathedral are placed in symmetrical balance. Symmetrical balance is formal balance. Informal or asymmetrical balance is the balance of objects which are not the same size or weight. By placing unequal objects at different distances from the center—the larger object nearer the center and the smaller object farther from the center—the same method of balance as the teeter board can be established. However, in architecture or decoration you are not working with weight alone but with apparent weight suggested by size, form, color, and even by texture. Thus a large object of indefinite form might be balanced by a smaller object of more decisive form. In color, a small but bright object will balance a larger dull-colored object, because the bright object will attract more atten-

tion. A pulpit and lectern, when of different size and design, can be made to balance asymmetrically by their position or distance from the center of the chancel or by the decoration of one and lack of decoration of the other.

All of the elements of design are dependent upon good spacing or proportion. In architecture, proportion is the relation of height to breadth and length. It has to do with the feeling one gets from a building. If we accept the fact that a building or room is more pleasing if it is longer than it is wide, we will want to know how to correct proportions that are not according to this standard. A room that is wide in comparison to its length can be altered by adding long horizontal lines of contrasting color or material to the side walls which will tend to make the side walls seem longer. Such a means might be used to correct the proportions of a square auditorium type of church.

Function or use will to a certain extent dictate the size and height of rooms, but we should never lose sight of the fact that the proportions of a room must please the eye. I know of a charming little church that was recently widened to give more seating space. However, in doing this the original proportions between the width and height were lost and the pleasing effect was also destroyed.

Proportions of a room should all be in the same ratio, that is, the height and length and width proportions of the windows and doors of a room should be in the same ratio as the all-over proportions of a room itself. If you want to decide on the correct size and shape of a platform or chancel, make it the same length and breadth proportionately as the length and breadth of the whole auditorium. Thus even the pleasing size for a pulpit can be determined by the ratio of its dimensions to those of the general over-all dimensions of the church chancel and nave. The architect will see to these proportions when the church is built. However, a carpenter or contractor often is called in to make changes in the size of a church, and this is done without consideration for the design and general appearance.

Scale in design refers to the unit of measure. In a building or room of large size the objects in

Massachusetts Institute of Technology Chapel, Cambridge, Massachusetts. The white marble altar has a halo of illumination from the lantern above the altar and a curtain of metal rectangles hung on rods. The wall behind the altar is red brick. Eero Saarinen, architect.

the room may also be large. This is especially true of churches where a heroic size scale may be chosen to help express man's longing to rise above the limitations of time and space. In small rooms we expect small scale, and if, instead, we find large furniture, we say it is out of scale, and thus it seems unpleasant and will also reduce the size of the room. Too large or too small, too high or too low a pulpit will seem to be out of scale. A painting or a piece of sculpture will often look wrong because it is out of scale with the church in which it is placed.

It is most important that a church give a unified impression. You should see it all at once as a work of art. A simple geometric form—a cube, a sphere, a cylinder—is unified. Buildings based on these simple forms, such as the cone of the Pyramid, the sphere of the Roman Pantheon, or the rectangle form of the Greek temple, possess unity. But few present-day buildings are so simple. However, to be beautiful in design, they must present a unified appearance.

Unity is created by a harmony of all parts and a subordination of all minor parts to one major element. In a church building a tower or dome can establish unity in the group of church buildings by tying them together. A tower of great height allows for no confusion as to which part

of the structure is for church services. But the tower is not the only way to dominate the design. This may be done by creating special interest. The church door can be made taller, wider, or more ornate than the door of the parish house. Curved lines and elements that suggest motion, such as steps, stairs, and gates, are more interesting than flat surfaces. All these diversities are allowed as long as they do not detract from the unity of the whole.

In the church interior, the chancel plan with the altar at the center makes a natural focal point to which all other parts of the structure can be unified. To help preserve this unity, the chancel is raised higher than the nave, and if it has steps, it is more interesting. Although there is no absolute rule about steps, the floor of the chancel should be at least one step above the floor of the nave; the floor of the sanctuary at least one step above the floor of the chancel; and the altar one or more steps above the sanctuary. For the sake of dominance, the altar should not only be large enough to attract attention, but should have a carved reredos, a large cross, a painting, or a dossal of damask to enrich and to hold the attention at the focal point. Sometimes the altar is small in comparison to the size of the church. It can be made to take an important place, however, by

First Universalist Church, Chicago. Stark simplicity marks this setting. The fabric screen back of the altar table is set in a steel frame, and the pulpit and lectern are of steel construction. The chancel floor is wood. The whole effect is that of beauty of line repetition. Schweikher and Elting, architects.

a certain harmony results. Unity of detail of decoration brings about harmony. Thus the Gothic choir stalls and chancel furniture echo the detail of fretwork in the Gothic window traceries. Unity can be attained through color harmony. All the colors should not only be harmonious in hue, but in intensity as well, as in a stained glass window. Building materials should be harmonious in color. They may contrast, but one material should dominate. Thus in using plaster and wood, or brick and stone, one material and one texture should dominate to give unity to the whole. But unity without variation is monotonous. There is no art without unity of design, but there must also be enough variety to give distinctive variations. All unity is dull, too much variety is confusing, but

St. Mark's Roman Catholic Church, Burlington, Vermont. The sculpture over the entrance is a seven-foot, six-inch aluminum crucifix on an oak cross, done by Charles Umlauf.

St. Mark's Episcopal Church, St. Louis, Missouri. One of the first contemporary churches built in the United States. The white brick exterior is painted off-white to match the limestone of the sculptured figure and the stone trim of the building. The lead flèche is partly covered with gold leaf. The richly panelled door is painted slate violet and the steps and terraced foreground with its limestone posts and iron chains make an impressive entrance. Nagel and Dunn, architects.

means of extra richness of design and color. The Riverside Church, New York City, is an example of a small altar given prominence by means of a bright gold elaborately designed candelabra which is spotlighted from above—and in contrast to the surrounding tracery of graystone. The space in which this altar stands is surprisingly narrow, but its color, design, and exaggerated height give it dominance. The general tendency of a building committee is to try to force the architect to sacrifice the aesthetic qualities of a roomy chancel and sanctuary so that "more people may be squeezed into the nave." This is one of the biggest mistakes that can be made.

Unity is also achieved by harmony of shapes. When all the windows are alike in height and width and all the spaces between windows equal,

it is unity in the variety that produces a dynamic work of art.

Monotony is caused by regular repetition of forms, uniformly spaced. On a monotonous structure with only surface ornament for variety no aesthetic values result. Much of the architecture of the Gothic Revival falls into this category. The builders used only the Gothic surface ornament and not the underlying spirit of the style. Thus a reproduction of a Gothic choir stall by means of present-day machinery and factory methods adds little to the decoration of a church. Better to have simple pews of good proportions and no attempt at decoration.

There should also be unity between the exterior and the interior of the church. How often we see a church which has an attractive exterior, but whose interior is so fancy and cluttered that it has no relation to its architectural structure. The nineteenth-century Roman Catholic church with its baroque interior decorations, plaster saints, and gilt decoration had no connection with its structural design. Fortunately, many of these churches are being redecorated and the fancy decorations and cheap plaster saints replaced with simple designs. If any votive figures are used in the Roman Catholic church today, usually they are of better design and workmanship, and often of quite modern design.

The Protestant churches have been slower to remedy the incongruity between the architecture and decoration of their churches. Where the nineteenth-century Roman Catholic Church erred with over-decoration, the Protestant Church of the last century generally erred from lack of interest and lack of color and decoration. Hundreds of Protestant churches were built with organ pipes, golden oak pews and pulpits, brass altar rails, and cheap glass windows with Sunday school card designs for decoration. Indeed, the average nineteenth-century church gave no recognition to the arts or to their contribution to the religious experience. Not until the last few years has church decoration recovered from these doldrums and finally begun to break through to the real depths of religious expression.

Structural unity between exterior and interior is expressed in an unpretentious modern church built of red brick. The interior also has red brick walls, floors, altar, and sanctuary rail. This is relieved by the varying textures of the different patterns of brick laying and by contrast with the wood of the rafters and pews and the blended lighting from the antique leaded English pot-glass.

When the feeling of organic or structural unity is missing, it is more noticeable in church architecture and decoration than it would be in any ordinary building—for in the church we expect perfection. There should be no second best.

Architect's model of St. Mark's Episcopal Church, St. Louis, Missouri, showing over-all master plan of buildings and grounds. The paved entrance court serves as outdoor narthex when weather permits. Nagel and Dunn, architects.

$$3$$

The Architectural Plan of the Church

THE traditional divisions of the nave, or space for the congregation, and the chancel and sanctuary, where the altar stands and the service takes place, are still essential divisions of the plan of the present-day liturgical church. These elements of the plan are usually enclosed in the traditional rectangular or cruciform building.

The cruciform or rectangular form of the liturgical church did not come into sudden being. It was determined by liturgy and tradition and evolved from the needs and requirements of the service of worship. It was also influenced by the places used for early Christian worship—the synagogue, the catacombs, and the basilica.

As the ritual grew more complex, more priests were required to conduct the service and more room was needed in the eastern end of the church. To provide the needed room, the building was projected from a rectangle to a cruciform, or the size of the apse was increased and eventually it evolved into the deep chancel of the Gothic church. Steps were added to raise the space so that the congregation could see the service.

The colonnade of arches stopped at the chancel and this factor together with the steps made a natural division between the chancel, where the service was conducted, and the nave, where the people stood or sat.

In the seventh century, when sprinkling took the place of immersion, the separate baptistry was no longer needed and after some years the font for baptism was set up in the narthex at the entrance to the church.

Thus through the ages the changing form of the church building was not determined so much by architectural considerations as by the growing complexity of the ritual.

By the end of the Middle Ages, the form of the liturgical church building was determined. The non-liturgical church, having relinquished the traditions, replaced the vestments with a black gown, stressed preaching, and did away with the altar. Thus there was no need for a chancel, and the non-liturgical church became a hall or meeting house with a speaker's desk.

The present-day trend in church architecture for most denominations is to restore the liturgical form with its traditional divisions of chancel, nave, and narthex. For this reason it seems best to consider the furnishing of the church according to the chancel plan. We will consider each division of the church separately, although to produce a satisfactory effect the church interior must be correlated and seen as a whole.

The chancel is the most important part of the church because the liturgical part of the service takes place there. The floor of the chancel is elevated from the nave for the sake of visibility and audibility. The ceiling of the chancel may be the same height as the nave ceiling or it may be higher. Added height gives more window space, more light, and greater dramatic effect.

The chancel in the typical liturgical plan usually includes the seats for the choir, the sanctuary behind whose altar rail is the altar itself, the sedilia, or fixed seats for the clergy, and the credence or aumbry. The furnishing of the altar is determined by church regulations and will be taken up in another chapter. Other architectural features of the chancel include the windows, the reredos, the altar rail, and the choir stalls. All of these chancel features should be a part of the architect's plan.

The Baptists and several other denominations

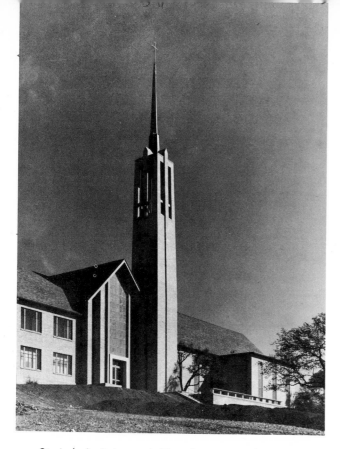

St. Luke's Episcopal Church, San Antonio, Texas. The stately tower and spire of contemporary design dominates the church exterior. Henry Steinbomer, architect.

conduct the service of baptism by immersion and thus need a baptismal pool. This baptismal pool is usually in the chancel. Also, the Baptist Church has in the past had a pulpit in the center of the chancel. Although the emphasis is still upon the preaching of the Gospel, the divided chancel plan with emphasis on baptism and communion has recently gained favor. The typical baptismal pool is lead lined on a wood sheathing and has two sets of stairs leading down into the water. The average depth of a baptismal pool is 3 feet 6 inches. Plans for a typical baptistry may be obtained from the American Baptist Home Mission Society, 164 Fifth Avenue, New York City.

The altar, its position, size, and the materials of which it is constructed should be planned by the architect and included in his initial design of the church. Not only is an altar an architectural feature, but being the center of interest, especially in all liturgical churches, it is an important fac-

tor determining the interior plan and decoration of the church. The altar stands in the sanctuary which is usually one step above the chancel and is enclosed by the altar rail. The altar itself should stand on a platform at least one, or as many as three, steps above the sanctuary floor.

The altar should be of such proportions and of such design that the attention is fixed on the rectangular form of the altar and not its fittings. Thus if the chancel itself has color and decoration the altar also should have richness. But it is important that the altar dominate and seem to stand out alone. For this reason it is not desirable to have the altar made of the same wood as the pews or wood panelling.

The size of the altar is partly determined by its use. That is, it must be a convenient height for the priest and it must be wide enough and long enough to hold the furnishings necessary for the service in the liturgical church, and for several priests to officiate at one time. For these purposes the altar should be thirty-nine and one-half inches in height, twenty-four to thirty-six inches in depth, and a minimum of six feet in length.

The liturgical or free-standing altar should stand out from the walls and should be finished on all four sides. The altar should have a platform or footpace at least forty inches wide. A retable or shelf above the altar is not considered proper. The majority of the factory-made altars shown in church furniture catalogues do not meet these measurement requirements. Some are only thirty-four inches high, a height which would be very inconvenient for a tall priest. Many have a depth of only the minimum twenty-four inches and some are only five feet in length.

The size of the altar is also determined by the size of the church as a whole. A large church requires a large altar and a small church or chapel will require an altar of smaller dimensions. The length and depth of the altar is also determined by the size of the chancel and by the proportions of the chancel. If the chancel is broad, it will need a longer altar than a narrow chancel. Also a deep chancel will need a deeper altar than a shallow chancel.

In the eleventh century, a decree ordered all altars to be made of stone, but this order was not always obeyed and there are altars of wood that date to the eleventh century. Many of these old altars were as short as three feet in length and might be fastened with brackets to the wall. Most stone altars were simple rectangular forms. From Elizabethan times down through the period of "Adam," wooden altars or Holy Tables followed the forms of the furniture of the period. We find English altars of Elizabethan times with carved bulbous legs, plain and severe Jacobean altars, ornate mahogany Chippendale altars, and typical Adam tables with fluted legs, carved acanthus, and medallion ornament.

Today, altars are made of stone such as sandstone and limestone or granite. The altar may also be made of brick or concrete either natural color or tinted. Altars are also made of marble of various colors. The imposing altar of St. Bartholomew's Church, New York City, is of dark green marble, while the simple buff sandstone altar of the Church of the Heavenly Rest, New York City, is equally impressive.

The material of which the altar is constructed will depend upon the style of the architecture, the size of the building, and the colors used in the decoration of the chancel and nave. A small simple church with red brick walls may have an altar of red brick, while a larger, more elaborate church might demand an altar of richer material and more sophisticated texture such as marble. In Corpus Christi Roman Catholic Church in San Francisco, the black marble altar contrasts with the dull red concrete walls and black and green asphalt tile floors.

For added decoration, the altar may be carved, painted, or inlaid with color and design. Wooden altars are usually made of oak, but may be constructed of walnut, mahogany, or any other hardwood. The wooden altar may be finished light or dark, with no added decoration, or it may be carved with a simple cross or IHS. Simple wooden altars are also made to be covered with frontals, changing colors with the church season.

The marble high altar in the Chapel of the Intercession, New York City, is unique in historical significance. It also presents an idea which could be followed in smaller churches. The front of the altar is a design of the "Jesse Tree," made up of a

mosaic of small stones gathered from places of early church worship. There are stones from Calvary, Bethlehem, Nazareth, the River Jordan, and other Bible places. There are also stones from well-known ancient churches such as Canterbury, Salisbury, and Westminster. Altogether the altar

Church of the Epiphany, Episcopal, New York City. This small church is Gothic in inspiration but contemporary in feeling. The tower rises above the chancel to give clerestory lighting, and the proportions are dramatic. The tall red and gold dossal rises above the stone altar. The tall cross and candlesticks are polychrome wood in gold and blue-green. William Rineland King, architect.

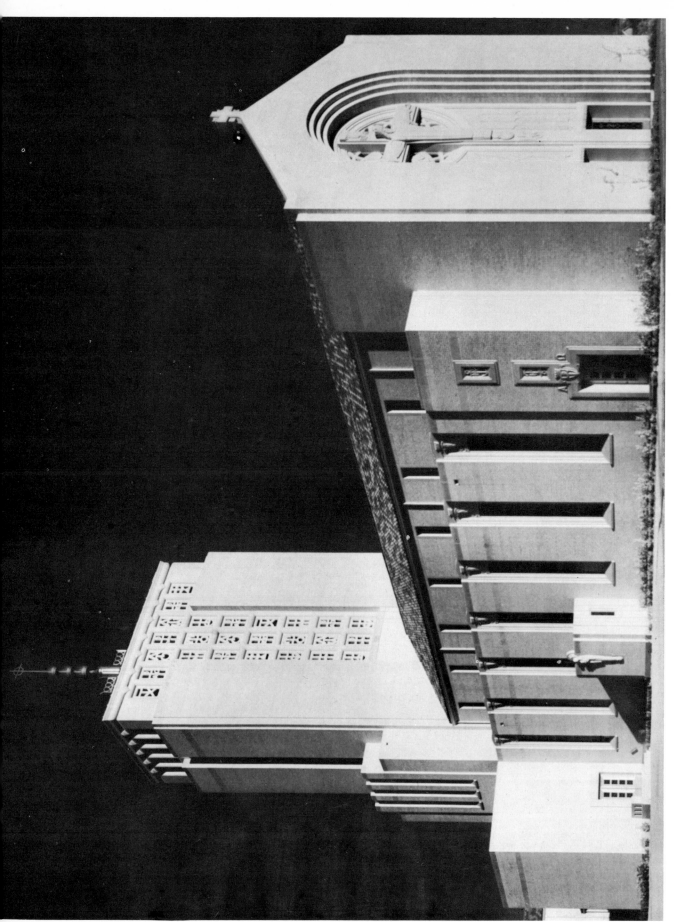

Church of Christ the King, Dallas, Texas. The impressive front facade is dominated by the huge stone carving of Christ the King by Ernest B. Haswell, sculptor. The huge tower is located over the sanctuary, providing clerestory light from its stained glass windows. The form of building defines interior liturgical divisions. Edward J. Schulte, architect.

contains 1,563 stones. These are held in place by a bronze vine springing from a central stem. Another interesting feature is the fact that each stone was given by a different parishioner so that all could have a part in the building of the altar. A list of each stone and its source is given in the church booklet.

The altar need not be a solid form, but can be a slab set on legs or pillars. Each altar slab or mensa should be consecrated with five incised crosses—one at the center and one at each corner. An altar should rest on a permanent surface such as stone, concrete, brick, or some other permanent material other than wood.

If there is a window behind the altar, the length of the altar is determined by the window. If there is a tall narrow window, the altar should be longer than the window. If the window is broad, or if there is a group of windows, the length of the altar should be within the outer lines of the window, but the altar must never be dwarfed in relation to the rest of the chancel.

The altar steps should be wide enough and the treads low enough so that the priest can conduct the services without danger of accidents. Also there should be a space of five or six feet between the lowest step of the altar and the altar rail so that several priests can pass back and forth when administering communion. There should again be five or six feet between the altar rail and the choir stalls, if the choir is in the chancel.

Whenever at all possible, an altar should be especially designed and custom made so that it fits the building not only in size but in harmony of color and materials.

Mail order altars should be the last resort. Better to have a simple pine altar made by the local carpenter than a stock design altar with cheap carving of pseudo-Gothic design or copybook inscriptions. Of all the church furniture catalogues that we have seen only one firm puts out a line of plain modern altars and furniture which might be suitable for the present-day church of simple good taste. Indeed, it is about time that the trade as well as the church building committees realized that Gothic is not the only answer to church furnishing! Today the wealthy city church, which, through memorials, can afford the craftsmanship of master carvers, sculptors, and stained glass workers that are so necessary to the expression of Gothic, is the only parish that should consider a Gothic-inspired church building.

The traditional decoration for the wall back of the altar was a reredos. A reredos was originally a moveable screen placed on a shelf and was changed with the seasons. This evolved into the lofty Gothic reredos constructed of stone with crocketed niches for figures, and tall pinnacles. Alabaster was also a favorite material for the reredos of the Middle Ages. In the seventeenth century, the reredos or altar screens were made of wood, classic in design, with Corinthian columns, a central pediment and carvings of garlands, scroll designs and vases and cherub heads. Over the altar were panels which held the Ten Commandments or the Lord's Prayer. The simplest form of reredos was a simple panel or panels with the Ten Commandments in the center and the Apostles' Creed on one side and the Lord's Prayer on the other. In St. Paul's Chapel, New York City, built in 1766, the Tables of Law are upheld by the glory of clouds and lightning.

There are also low altar pieces which include a painting, or mosaic, or a carved wooden or stone panel depicting the Last Supper, the Annunciation, the Nativity, the Ascension, or other scenes from the life of Christ. Another form of altarpiece is the triptych which is composed of three panels and may be painted in polychrome and gold or may be of carved wood. The panels should be made to close during Lent and their backs should be painted in a plain neutral color.

The reredos or altar screen may be the same length as the altar or it may extend to cover most of the space of the eastern chancel wall. The wall behind the altar may be hung with a dossal and the colors changed with the church seasons. In the little church of St. Paul's-in-the-Desert, Palm Springs, California, a permanent sky blue dossal is painted on the stucco wall behind an altar and platform of rose-colored cast cement. Marble stencilled with a pattern of gold leaf forms the background for the altar at the Church of the Ascension, New York City. Above this is the famous La Farge painting of the Ascension. The liturgical dossal with its colors changing with the church

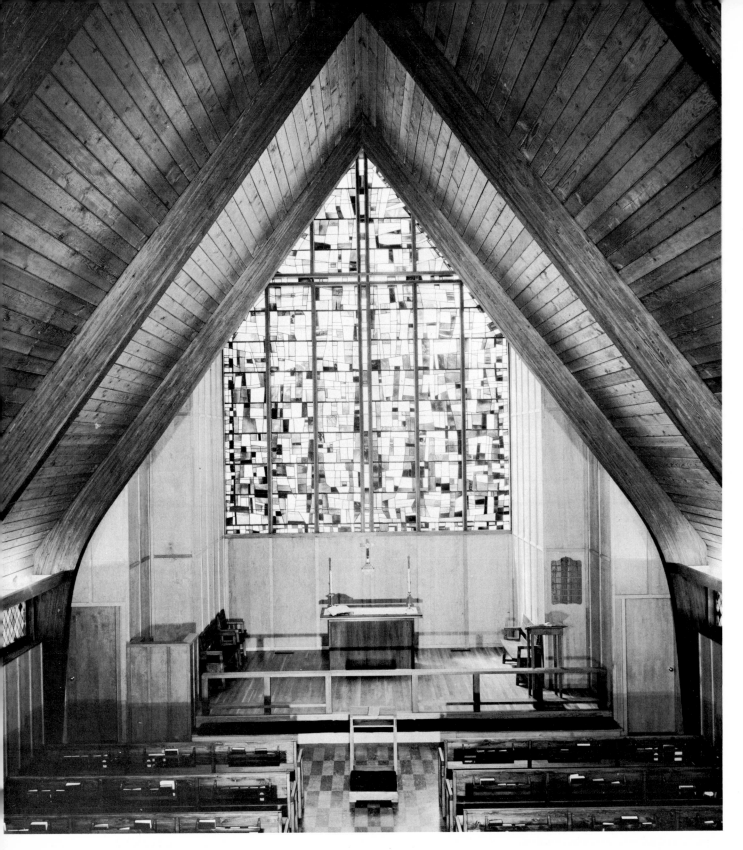

St. George's Episcopal Church, Durham, New Hampshire. The abstract design of stained glass in orange-reds, yellows, purples, and green gives warmth and atmosphere to the simple interior of laminated beams and pine panellings. The chancel holds the altar, lectern, and pulpit. The organ and choir are in the rear. John A. Carter, architect.

34

feasts will be treated in detail later.

Many modern churches are designed with the effective austerity of the monastery chapel. These have a prominent cross or crucifix set against a wall of contrasting material, or the whole eastern chancel wall may be of glass with a large cross over the altar as part of the design worked in glass. A large cross or crucifix should always be made according to the architect's specifications as to design, size, and materials.

The altar rail, although not so important to the architecture of the building, is one of the features prescribed by the liturgy and so must be included in the plan of the liturgical church. The present form of the altar rail, either across the chancel or on three sides of the altar, was determined in the eighteenth century after much liturgical controversy. Altar rails should be designed by the architect and not put in as an afterthought. A simple temporary rail may be replaced by a more expensive rail when money is available. Altar rails may be of stone, marble, brick, cast concrete, wood, or metals. The altar rail may be a stationary part of the architecture or it may be separately constructed. In the nineteenth century, brass altar rails were popular, but they now require too much upkeep because of the polishing necessary. Wrought iron, wood, bronze, or aluminum are more satisfactory today.

The space for the choir presents a problem in the modern church. The chancel stalls were originally occupied by extra priests. Indeed, important as the vested choir is today, it did not move to its position in the chancel until near the middle of the nineteenth century. Before that time both choir and organ were in the gallery at the other end of the nave or in the loft above the rood screen. When a choir takes part in the service by chants and responses, it seems natural that they be placed nearer the altar. If the choir is in the chancel, a wide chancel is necessary so that the choir does not obtrude on the altar and detract from the service. The choir seats should be low and as concentrated to the sides of the chancel as possible. However, the trend today is to move the choir back to the west gallery.

Although the rood screen or division wall between the chancel and the nave has been done away with, many churches retain the rood beam with its cross or crucifix and often the figures of the Virgin and St. John set on the beam.

The two important liturgical requirements of the nave are the pulpit and the lectern. The importance of the pulpit varies with the denomination of the church. The pulpit of a large church or a cathedral becomes an architectural factor, while the pulpit of a small church may be classified as furniture. The pulpit in some Protestant churches is considered as important as the altar.

The position of the pulpit was subject to change down through the ages. Many pulpits particularly in the eighteenth century were in front and above the altar. Examples of this type of pulpit still exist in St. James' Church, Goose Creek, South Carolina, and in St. Michael's, Charleston, South Carolina. However, the accepted place for the pulpit of the present-day liturgical church is in the nave to the side of the chancel. In medieval churches, the pulpit ranked second only to the altar or font. The best craftsmen were chosen for its construction, and whether the pulpit was of stone or wood it was richly and beautifully carved or painted. Many pulpits were octagonal in plan and divided into panels, with heavy cornices with carved tracery or figures. The pulpit also had a base and winding stairs leading from the floor of the nave and a canopied tester above to aid the sound and for more decoration. If you are building a large church and have the money for an elaborate pulpit, there is plenty of literature and illustrations of traditional pulpits.

The lectern or reading desk is placed on the opposite side of the nave and is simpler in design and smaller than the pulpit. The eagle lectern was a favorite design, but correctly should only be used for the reading of the Gospel. Both the lectern and the pulpit will be considered in the chapter on church furniture.

After the architect has laid out the plans according to the liturgical requirements of a church, the design of the structure will come almost unconsciously, for here he can rely on his own inventiveness and originality. Unless he is building a church in a traditional style of architecture, such features as the doors, windows, the height and design of the walls, and the proportions of the building are limited only by the general plan, the money available, the size of the site, and the limitations of his own talent.

One of the important architectural features of a church is the entrance door. It must be of pleasing design and ample size. The entrance door offers a place to spend extra money to good effect. Fine mouldings, handworkmanship, a bit of craftsmanship on the lock, or even a coat of welcoming red paint will give a church door warmth and character.

A doorway may be given accent and distinction by a pediment over the door, or it may have a window above the door. The door may be recessed in an archway, or a series of archways, or it may have a portico of columns as do many of the New England churches. Doors can also be made important by the use of contrasting materials and colors. Thus a brick church may have a white wooden door or a stone frame about the doorway. A stucco church may have a brick or a stone doorway. A cross may be placed above the door. The door itself may have a pattern of studded nails or an extra large knocker and lock.

For practical purposes, a church door must be wide enough to allow two persons to walk side by side carrying a casket. The minimum space needed is five and one-half feet. The center church aisle should be the same width and the side aisles should be wide enough for two persons to march side by side.

Rows and columns and archways so important in churches of traditional architectural styles are no longer necessary to church buildings. First of all, they are not required by the service or for the feeling of religious tone or dignity of the building. An atmosphere conducive to worship can be produced as well by more simple architecture and at less expense.

Windows play a different role in the twentieth-century church. In the past, windows were usually set in a formal arrangement of one or two tiers on each side of the church or there were rows of clerestory windows filled with stained glass. The windows in the chancel usually consisted of one or a group of Gothic stained glass windows in the Gothic church or a three-part Palladian window in the church of classic design. These windows were usually of small rectangular panes of clear glass.

The sanctuary of St. Bartholomew's Episcopal Church, New York City. The altar is of malachite green marble, the candelabra are bronze, and the clergy seats are of marble. The wall and pavement decorations are by Hildreth Meiere. Dignity of design is gained by full proportion.

St. George's Church and Friary, Roman Catholic, Seattle, Washington. An example of monastic simplicity with good proportion and subordination of all elements, which serves to emphasize the altar. Paul Thiry, architect.

Windows are still an important architectural feature of churches today, but instead of the formal arrangement the window space is often concentrated to one wall. Thus the church may have a wall of windows or glass brick on one side only, or the chancel may have a wall of small-paned windows at one side so that the rays of light give a dramatic effect as they fall across the altar. In such a design, there may be windows in the chancel only, with solid walls in the nave. Or the only windows may be skylights. Several modern churches have been constructed with all the walls of glass. This is satisfactory where the glass is opaque or where a design filters the light so that the attention is concentrated on the altar and not out of the windows. A window behind the altar, that makes the outdoors the background for the altar, does not solve the problem of the purpose of the church. The church should be a setting for the act of the worship of God. The outdoor setting, unless through diffused glass, makes us nature worshippers, and those who want to contemplate nature need not come into the sanctuary of a church to do so.

The design and decoration of the walls of the present day are architectural problems that should be left to the architect. There are no liturgical limitations on wall treatment and there should be no dictation based on the tastes of the building committee. The interior walls of a church may be of any material—stone, wood, brick, plaster, marble, or even glass. In the medieval and Renaissance church, walls were decorated with sculpture and carvings in stone or wood. Color was not necessary because the surface was enriched by pattern. In the nineteenth-century era of church building, most walls were of plaster and seemed to require painted decoration.

Painted decoration has now become less important, for the modern church depends upon structural values and the beauty of natural materials and good proportions. Color is now used in large areas on walls rather than in intricate patterns and this serves to organize the architectural elements. Thus one wall may be of one color or of one material, such as plaster, while another wall may be fieldstone, and a third wall or portion of wall may be of glass. The walls of a church nave may be of gray stone while the walls of the chancel which should focus more attention may be painted flame color with a simple aluminum cross hung on the wall behind a gray marble altar. Walls which have plain, undecorated surfaces must be of fine proportions, and the spaces left between doors and windows must be pleasing in shape and a part of the design rather than nondescript spaces.

In redecorating an old church, the color of the wall can help to correct unpleasing proportions. It can be used to lengthen or shorten distances or to raise or lower a ceiling. Long lines of contrasting color converging at the eastern end of the nave give a feeling of length. A contrast of color in the wall, such as a wainscot or a change in color above a moulding can break the height of a ceiling, while a plain wall of one tone will make the ceiling seem higher and the room darker. The color of the wall can do more than anything else to lighten or darken a church. Thus dark panelled woodwork can be bleached or painted to lighten a dark church which has few windows.

In rebuilding an old church, it is a mistake to try to change the style of the building. Instead, the structure must be made the best of its present type. This will not only cost less, but also result in a better looking church.

Before making any changes in an old church, check the proportions. It may be too long for its width or too wide or too low for its length. If the oppressiveness of wrong proportions is removed, you have gone a long way in improving the building. You may find you need to change the level of the ceiling. A slanting floor may want to be flattened out, or some windows may need to be blanked out.

You may not need new pews, but the spacing and arrangement of the pews may need to be changed. You may find, also, the need for alterations in the form or arrangement of other furniture such as the pulpit or lectern. You may need a new altar or communion table.

You may need to take out or replace old painted glass windows. Or you may need a new lighting system. An effective lighting system can go far to remedy the faults of a dark gloomy church. Or you may need to change the color scheme to lighten the church or to replace the wrong use of colors that clash with each other. In fact, a good color scheme can go far toward bringing the old church out of the doldrums. When making any of these changes, an expert decorator or architect should be found to supervise the job.

A word should be said about two radical trends in modern ecclesiastical architecture. One is the church built to house the revival of the ancient custom of the priest facing the congregation for the eucharist, and this necessitates an altar set out from the wall. This requires extra space in the chancel, and the choir must be moved to the gallery or to an enclosed space behind the free standing altar. Another concept of modern church building might be called the church-in-the-round with the altar in the center and the people facing the altar and also facing each other. Both Roman Catholic and Protestant churches have been built on this plan. An altar rail surrounds the altar on all four sides and a cross or crucifix is suspended above the altar. The pulpit lectern is on one side and the font at the other.

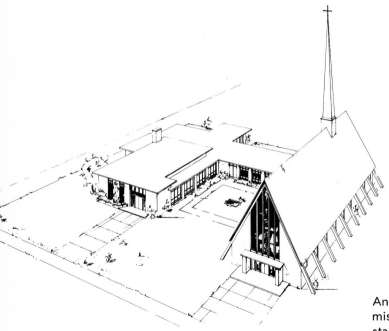

An architect's drawing of a frame mission church to be built in four stages. Maurice R. Salo, architect.

4

The Baptismal Font

In ancient days, the font was housed in a separate building called the baptistry. This building was usually built over a well or pool and baptism was by immersion. When baptism by affusion or sprinkling became the general rule, the font took its present location and form—a bowl on a shaft set upon a base. Today the font is usually located within the porch or narthex and is the first object within a church to attract attention. The font is set up near the entrance door as a reminder that baptism is the entrance into the Christian life.

In some churches, fonts are placed in the chancel. The Lutheran church places the font in front of the altar, while other Protestant denominations have no stationary font but use a silver bowl held by the minister. In Reformation days, an iron ring was often attached to the altar to hold this bowl when not in use.

When the font is placed within the chancel as it is in many churches, it is usually of smaller dimensions than the font at the entrance to the church. The chancel font should not interfere with the altar. For this reason it is usually placed to the side and front and just inside the altar rail. When the font is placed at the chancel end of the church, more space is left for pews and general circulation at the church entrance. The placement of the font in the chancel emphasizes the two ordinances of baptism and communion. Denominations still using baptism by immersion make provisions for pools under the chancel floor.

A review of the types of fonts used in England from Norman times down to the nineteenth century will give an interesting picture of the shapes, the materials, and the decoration of the font.

Early Norman fonts were cylindrical, or tub-like, or square in shape, and were made of stone or lead. They were decorated with carvings of arcaded pillars and arches and bands of Celtic interlacing borders or cable or zig-zag ornament. Sometimes there were quaint human figures or grotesque animal carvings. Early fonts were also rectangular in shape, but from the time of Henry III the font bowl was usually octagonal, or hexagonal. Many old capitals of columns served as

The simple, but dignified, solid stone baptismal font of St. James' Episcopal Church, New York City. The polychrome and gold wood cover opens to form a colorful background. The candlesticks are also wood polychrome.

Christ Lutheran Church, Minneapolis, Minnesota. The baptismal font is of ebony and stainless steel, set on a marble base. Eliel and Eero Saarinen, architects.

fonts. In medieval times, the font form evolved as a bowl with stem and base. Sometimes this form is also supported by four outside columns.

The Gothic font was polygonal in shape and was decorated with Gothic arches and tracery and with naturalistic foliage and figure decoration. In the late seventeenth and early eighteenth centuries, Inigo Jones and Sir Christopher Wren designed graceful fonts which were like vases set on pillars. These fonts were of marble or of wood with a silver bowl fitted inside to hold the water.

The canonical material prescribed for the font was stone and many fonts were made of stone, granite, and various types and colors of marble. A dark marble called Tournai marble and green Cornish Catacleuse were popular marbles. Fonts were also made of artificial stone and brick, and of such metals as lead, brass, pewter, and iron.

In addition to the types of design already described, fonts were decorated with pictorial subjects such as the Baptism of our Lord, the Adoration of the Magi, the Creation, the Subjugation of the Powers of Evil, the Massacre of the Innocents, the Flight into Egypt, the Last Supper, the Crucifixion, and the Descent from the Cross. The Seven Sacraments were carved on the sides of octagonal fonts, with the eighth panel depicting the Crucifixion. Symbolic animals such as the fish, doves, the serpent, and the lion were also frequent motifs of decoration. The Four Evangelists' heads were sometimes sculptured around the bowl, or their symbols—the angel for St. Matthew, the lion for St. Mark, the ox for St. Luke, and the eagle for St. John—might be used. Other sculptured subject matter included the signs of the zodiac, and the emblems of the months. Some fonts were marked with scripture quotations such as Ephesians 4:5, "There is one Lord, one Faith, one Baptism." Other suitable quotations used included Psalms 42:1, 121:1, or 122:1; Matthew 28:19; and Mark 16:16. Fonts were also marked with the names of donors, and were given with the request of prayers for the soul of the donor.

Whatever the decoration used on the font, there are also practical considerations such as a cover.

The font should have a cover to keep the water clean. In medieval times the cover was locked to prevent any superstitious use of the consecrated water. The earliest font covers were flat wooden lids. Gradually the cover assumed the dome shape, then the ogee-shaped canopy, and finally in the fifteenth century the tall spire-like cover with crockets and pinnacles of elaborately carved stone or wood. Font covers of seventeenth- and eighteenth-century Renaissance design were made of mahogany or some other hardwood carved with Renaissance borders and swags of fruit and flowers and often surmounted by a carved pineapple or a blaze.

The font is usually raised on a small stand or platform, but it may be raised on several steps to give it a more impressive setting. Ample standing space for the priest should be made on the top step. A font may also be placed in a niche with the wall behind it decorated with some suitable subject carved, painted, or executed in tile or glass mosaic or colorful enamel.

The dimensions of the baptismal font are important for the convenience of the priest. The recommended height is thirty-nine and one-half inches and the inside diameter with its removable metal liner should be at least fifteen inches. A simple flat metal or wooden cover is sufficient. In a church of modern design a cast concrete font of fine proportions or a simple basin on an iron or aluminum stand can be made as effective as a more expensive font. Present-day fonts are also designed of wood or may be made of brick or of a plain shaft of colored marble. A stone bowl may stand on a shaft of stone and have a metal or wooden cover.

Many present-day fonts are given as memorials and as such have their own setting in a chantry chapel or in a separate baptistry chapel. The Second Congregational Church of Newton, Massachusetts, has such a chapel as do St. Bartholomew's Church and Grace Church, New York City. The font in the Brick Presbyterian Church, New York City, is placed at the entrance to the chapel. A font in a chapel has the advantage of intimacy and also provides seats for those witnessing the ceremony.

Wherever the font is placed, it should have an important position and by its design and decorative setting should proclaim itself as an important part of the church. The font is second only to the

St. Anthony's Roman Catholic Church, Fort Lauderdale, Florida. The wrought iron gates provide a simple setting for the green Italian marble baptismal font with stainless steel cover. Rambusch Decorating Co.

altar in liturgical significance and should be the starting place of the dynamic progression from the entrance of the church to the final climax of architectural focus, the altar. A good, simply designed font in harmony with the architecture of the rest of the church will supply the dignity needed. In a small redwood or cedar church, the font might be of terra cotta brick, or it might be of aluminum with decorative accents of black lacquer or even plastic.

If the architect cannot design a font and if there is no local cabinetmaker to build one, perhaps it will be necessary to order the font from a catalog of church furniture. Most church furniture manufacturers make fonts. They are usually of oak and can be ordered in several different finishes. The average commercial font has some carving and unfortunately most of it still is Gothic in design. When a church must buy a commercial font, the one selected should be as simple as possible with a few well-spaced mouldings. Commercial fonts are made with stainless metal bowls. These should be removable, and not made with a

41

drain. The water should be taken to the sacristy piscina or poured on the earth. Tall font covers are expensive, and a flat wooden or metal cover with a ring or small cross as a handle is satisfactory. A silk dossal may hang on the wall back of the font and a pair of pavement candlesticks will help to give an impressive setting. However, the ideal setting is to have the font placed in an alcove or niche separated from the rest of the building by a grille of wrought iron, aluminum, bronze, or wood. The font itself may be marble set on a base of a different color marble and the cover may be bronze. A shaft of green marble set on black marble with a cover of bronze makes a dignified font. A stone shaft with a bowl and cover of bronze is also suitable. A shaft of green marble with a copper base and bowl makes a distinctive font. If the floor is of lighter green terrazzo and the space

closed in by wrought iron gates, it will make a suitable font for either a traditional or contemporary church. The gates of the small baptistry may be designed with symbols such as the fish or cross or may be of simple geometric design.

Whatever the design of the font, it should always be distinctive, and if the font itself lacks distinction, its setting may be made to emphasize its important purpose.

In rebuilding an old church, a stained glass window that does not fit into the expanded size of the nave could be used in the baptismal niche. Permanent materials such as stone and marble give dignity and importance. These enduring and monumental materials should not be forgotten, and in our present-day rush to create church space we should also build church buildings which will endure for years to come.

St. Luke's Chapel, Clarkson Memorial Hospital, Omaha, Nebraska. Entrance doors of glass with blasted design of cross and crown. Baptismal font of contemporary design marble with metal top. Rambusch Decorating Co.

5

Floors and Floor Coverings

Floors, together with the walls and ceiling, constitute the architectural background of the church building. The floor is also a part of the foundation of the building and as such should be solid and strong and give a feeling of permanence. The flooring materials should be harmonious with the other structural materials of the building and should be of the best quality that can be afforded.

Both the flooring material and the floor treatment or covering should be decided upon when the initial plans for the church are being made. Do you want a floor covering of carpet, or do you want a permanent floor of structural material which will also serve as a part of the decorative scheme? Do you want the floor used as background, or do you want a decorative floor? These are questions that should be discussed in consultation with the architect, because expert advice is needed.

If carpeting is to be used, the decision should be made prior to the time when the architect and the acoustical consultant are starting the preliminary architectural plan since carpeting and pew cushions affect the acoustical properties of a church.

Since the floor is the foundation it should be darker in tone than the walls or ceiling. This distribution of tone makes the floor "keep its place" and balances the whole decorative scheme of the room. Floor coverings such as rugs may be lighter, and floor accents such as decorative tiles or mosaics may also be lighter in tone than the floors as a whole. The floor as the foundation of the building and as a part of the background of the decorative scheme should be related to the walls in both tone and color. In tone it should be darker than the walls and ceiling and in color the background floor should be less intense or grayer than the walls. When the floor is decorative, there may be more variety in tone and color, but even then it is more satisfactory if the floor remains darker in relation to the walls. Decorative floors are floors with pattern, whether it be in the structure of the floor, such as inlaid marble or mosaic, or in the floor covering, such as an oriental rug or patterned carpet.

Down through the ages churches have had floors of brick, tile, slate, marble, or hand-hewn wood. The majority of these old floors have lasted the test of time. Some old churches have floors of inscribed stones which cover graves under the church. Many Victorian churches were built with aisles and chancel floors of ceramic tiles laid in geometric patterns or of marble mosaics with colorful borders.

Wood is the most widely used flooring material. Pine, maple, or oak floors are both good-looking and durable. They should be well laid with tongue-and-groove so that there are no cracks between the boards. A cheap wood floor requires a covering which in turn demands more upkeep and replacement, while a good hardwood floor will last many years. The better the workmanship and materials, such as hand-hewn boards, the less the maintenance costs. In a building of frame construction the wooden floor is most practical; also it can be used with a less costly under girder than floors of such material as marble and flagstone.

In some church buildings of stone contruction, marble floors are suitable. Marble floors require no covering, they will last forever, and they are easy to keep clean. Marble is available in colorings of grays, browns, or greens, all suitable for floors. Marble may also be laid in black and white checks and other geometric patterns or in elab-

Holy Cross Lutheran Church, Wichita, Kansas. The masonry walls are of reddish brown brick. The parabolic form ceiling is of tongue-and-grooved planks. The floor is green asphalt tile and the aisle is carpeted. The translucent plastic panel above the chancel gives a soft light. The large hanging cross is of laminated redwood, carved by Bernard Frazier. There will be a ceramic mosaic in the curved recess on the chancel wall. The stone slab of the altar is of Minnesota granite. Ramey and Himes, architects.

44

orate designs. A plain marble floor is suitable in the nave of the church while a more elaborate floor of marble laid in appropriate design may be used in the chancel and in the sanctuary near the altar. Marble floors may also have borders or medallions of mosaics. However, the weight of a marble floor demands a reinforced support, and marble is the most expensive flooring.

Terrazzo, which is a combination of marble chips and cement, is also a lifetime flooring. It is suitable for a church of stone construction and also frame buildings, especially in warm climates where it can be poured on a wood or flat concrete surface when there is no basement. Terrazzo costs about one fourth of the price of marble and is kept clean with clear water mopping and occasional buffing. Terrazzo gains gloss and beauty with use and can be made in any color combination to harmonize with structural materials and the decorative scheme of the church. Terrazzo floors can be made dark or light to harmonize and to accent any color scheme. A combination of black and white marble chips gives a simple neutral flooring, but many tones of brown, green, and even pink are available. Terrazzo can be mixed in almost as many varieties of color and tone as paint. Because of its great decorative value and comparatively low cost, terrazzo should be used much more than it is in present-day churches.

Ceramic tile, while it does not offer the wide choice of colors of terrazzo and costs slightly more, makes a satisfactory flooring for a church because it takes hard wear. It is thus particularly suitable for the narthex and central aisle. Terra-cotta tiles in large squares give a floor stability and they seem to "stay down." Several churches in New York City, including St. Thomas Episcopal Church, have floors of large square terra-cotta tiles. Such tiles would also be fitting in a small church of wood construction.

Flagstone is another permanent material for church floors. After laying, the flagstone is treated with a filler to seal it against spots and then is kept in condition by waxing. A flagstone exterior entrance, narthex, and central aisle is often combined with wooden flooring in the pew areas.

Flagstone is available in many attractive colors: blue, gray, buff, brown, blue-green, green, lilac, and rust. Flagstone may be laid in squares of one color for the church narthex and aisles, while the floor of the chancel and sanctuary could have a simple design of two tones of the stone. Vermont slate is available in vivid reds, greens, and purple. New York and Pennsylvania blue stone is gray, while Tennessee flagstone comes in browns, tans, pinks, and stripes or veinings of several tones of brown. Western or Arizona flagstone is usually in tones of pink or tan. While these various colors are available to harmonize with most any color scheme, the less expensive and sensible solution is to use the stone native to the locality where the church is being built.

Travertine is another type of flooring that is suitable for church flooring. It comes in tones of tan and is laid in large rectangular slabs. It is easy to walk on and long lasting. It is cleaned with soap and water and the cost is below that of marble. It gives a mellow appearance and is less formal than marble.

A properly laid concrete floor is also durable. It is ideal for a basement floor or can be made attractive with rubber-base masonry paint. It can later be carpeted or covered with terrazzo or a floor covering of asphalt tile or some other resilient flooring.

When the flooring of the church has not been planned with the decorative scheme in mind, it may be necessary to choose a floor covering. For example, a church with a wooden floor may seem bare and need carpeting for the center aisle and chancel, or some resilient floor covering may be used to help give warmth and color. Resilients have the advantage of economy and easy maintenance, but in the opinion of this writer seldom offer the dignity necessary for the church proper, although they are suitable for offices, Sunday school rooms, and recreational rooms.

Linoleum is one of the cheapest resilient floor coverings and is available in rolls or tiles. It can be kept in condition with a thin coat of wax which should be removed and rewaxed from time to time. It ranges from 20¢ to 30¢ per square foot in price.

Asphalt tile gives long service and is easy to install and requires little maintenance. It should be waxed and cleaned with soapsuds and water.

Danforth Chapel, Colorado A. & M. College, Fort Collins, Colorado. Random lengths and heights of natural stone walls and flagstone floors add to the rustic effect of this contemporary chapel by James A. Hunter, architect. Cross, Communion rail, and altar appointments by Lynn Wolfe.

The cost, from 10¢ to 25¢ per square foot, is even lower than the price of good linoleum. Vinyl asbestos tile is more expensive, as is rubber tile—ranging from 30¢ to 60¢ per square foot.

Cork tile gives a good-looking flooring. It comes in tones of brown and can be laid in geometric squares and rectangles to form a pattern. It is not cheap since the prices range from 45¢ to 80¢ per square foot. It also requires frequent cleaning and waxing and doesn't stand hard wear, although vinyl cork wears better than plain cork.

Vinyl plastic tile will keep its appearance for many years with a minimum of upkeep which offsets its higher initial cost which is from 75¢ to $1 per square foot.

Of course the handsomest floor coverings are rugs or carpets. Carpet is sound-absorbent and thus has acoustic value. However, it requires regular sweeping and cleaning and replacement every few years. Good quality carpets suitable for churches range from $11 per square yard up. The range of color in plain carpets is almost unlimited and any tone from light to dark is also available. Also there are many weaves and textures as well as sculptured surfaces to choose from. The most suitable carpet for the church is one that is of one color or possibly two tones of one color. This may be a solid plain carpet or one with a simple all-over repeat pattern.

Wilton carpet is the most satisfactory type of carpet for the church. It looks best and lasts longest. Wilton carpet can be had with both cut and loop pile and in several widths. The cut pile gives the best wear. In price, Wilton carpets suitable for use in churches range from $11 a square yard up. Plain Wiltons are made in one or two tone effects and also in figures. Simple shell or scroll or Gothic arch patterns or any small all-over repeat patterns are suitable for church use.

A carpet with a round wire weave is also satisfactory for church use. It is woven in 9-foot widths, but has a seam-lock so that no seam joinings are visible. Round wire weave carpet is made in plain and moresque effect patterns and sells for about $11 per square yard.

Heavy twist carpet of "nugget" weight is also durable for church use. It is made in widths of 9, 12, 15, and 18 feet. Worsted brussels carpet is also durable for church use. It is made in many small all-over designs suitable for different types of churches.

Plain velvet carpet can be custom made in any size or any color. It wears well but is expensive, costing from $15 per square yard up. High pile textures are not suitable for church use since they crush with heavy traffic and, if looped, the loops have a tendency to pull.

Generally speaking, a plain or small figured car-

Stained glass window by Emil Frei in Danforth Chapel, Colorado A. & M. College, Fort Collins, Colorado.

Chapel of the Reformed Faith, Brick Presbyterian Church, New York City. The Celtic cross, richly carved and ornamented with gold, red, and blue polychrome, hangs above the altar against a deep blue velvet curtain. The surrounding woodwork is brown oak with a carved polychrome cornice. The chancel rail is of wrought iron and brass. The floor is of Virginia greenstone. At the foot of the Verde antique marble steps is a mosaic of the rising sun and the crest of Geneva. Adams and Woodbridge, architects.

pet is most suitable for the church, but wide aisles in a large church can take a larger pattern if it does not draw undue attention.

When floor coverings are used as decoration, the Oriental rug, either antique or modern, is in keeping with the ecclesiastical atmosphere. Oriental rugs are woven in conventional patterns, and their colors are also harmonious with those in stained glass windows and with the seasonal colors of church use. Oriental rugs may be used in the chancel or on the sanctuary steps or as a footpace rug before the altar. They add color and richness to the setting. All types of Oriental rugs are long wearing and do not show dirt or hard wear. Orientals come in many sizes, although no two are exactly the same size. There are large orientals which would cover a chancel floor and runners of various widths and lengths which would fit the altar steps. Other rugs are narrow enough to be used as footpace rugs. The best modern orientals are the domestic Karastans. These rugs are usually copies of antique orientals in color and pattern. They have the advantage of a heavier even surface pile. They are available in 9 by 12 feet, 9 by 15 feet, 9 by 18 feet, 10½ by 12 feet, 10½ by 14 feet, 10½ by 16 feet, 12 by

12 feet, and many other sizes so that they would fit most any chancel or sanctuary.

Rugs of handmade needlework with symbolical religious designs such as the emblems of the apostles or saints or crosses or church monograms are particularly effective for the sanctuary or the footpace at the altar. Rug patterns in these appropriate patterns and with proper colorings can be designed to order at many needlework shops, and if there are women in the church guilds who can do such work, nothing can be more suitable for the sanctuary than such a rug.

Carpets and rugs should be tried in the place where they are to be used, since both position and lighting will affect the color and pattern. The bright light of the showroom is altogether different from the dim light in the average church.

The important thing in a rug or carpet is the evenness of its surface. The pattern must not seem to project above the floor surface. To create this feeling of stability, the forms and colors must be of equal tone value with each other. The pat-terns and colors must be equally distributed. Strong color contrasts destroy the impression of flatness.

The general tendency today is to carpet the church. It gives it a feeling of warmth and comfort. Carpet is much cheaper than a fine marble or stone floor. However, in using carpet in the church instead of a permanent structural floor of material related to the architecture, we make the floor a part of the interior decoration and not a functional architectural factor. The carpeted church also does not have the same dignity and monumental quality of the church whose flooring is of strong, enduring, structural material. However, in a church that is comparatively bare of ornament and color, a carpet of some such color as red, gold, green, or terra cotta laid in the center aisle and up the steps leading to the altar may be effective. If, on the other hand, there should be polychrome decorations or a painted reredos or enameled cross, the strong color carpet will detract from the other decorations.

St. Anthony's Church, Nepera Park, New York. A brick arch separates the sanctuary from the nave of the church. A strip of colored mosaic carries the eye down the aisle to the sanctuary. Mosaic also forms the outline of the large cross set in the off-white sanctuary wall. The six low relief panels below the arms of the cross are the work of Hugh Maurin. The painted glass windows are the work of André Girard. J. Sanford Shanley, architect.

Lutheran Church of Our Redeemer, Los Angeles, California. A mural of Christian symbolism forms the background of the sanctuary. The Christus Rex cross was carved by Karel Pechance. The vine mural was executed by Mario de Ferrante. The altar is of Cordova shellstone. The color scheme is in greens, golds, and grays, with accents of red. The wooden ceiling is stained blue-green, and light from above the sanctuary floods the altar with beams of gold. Chaix and Johnson, architects.

50

6

Color in Church Decoration

IN ITS finest periods of architecture, the Church has used both color and ornament. Even the early Christians worshipping secretly in the catacombs of Rome painted colorful symbols of their religion on the walls of their place of worship.

The Roman basilica type church was a long hall with marble columns and a wooden roof with a coffered pattern. The floor was made of marble scraps set in colorful patterns and was the chief color decoration of the building. However, during a service the pillars of the marble baldachin were hung with richly embroidered and brocaded hangings, and the vestments of the priests gave rich color and ornament.

The Byzantine church, with its circular dome, was decorated with colorful mosaics. Red, blue, orange, and green mosaics, with occasional uses of black and white, sparkled on the gold backgrounds and brought color and warmth into the bare, practically windowless, buildings. The subject matter of these mosaics was related to the service of the church.

The next development in church architecture was the Romanesque. The vital principle of Romanesque architecture was the round-headed arch. The stone vaulted roof and the windows were round-headed. The walls were thick and solid, with a few apertures, and the proportions of width and height gave a certain heaviness in spite of the towers. Romanesque churches were dark—too dark for painting—and the favorite form of decoration was the bas-relief. Although Romanesque sculpture was abstract and conventional, the patterns gave a play of light and shade and thus enriched the surface of the stone. For color, again the church service employed rich hangings of gold and brilliant color, and the vestments of the priests repeated the color harmonies.

The Gothic church with its high, pointed arches and many open spaces vies with the Byzantine for beauty of color. The brilliance of the tall, stained glass windows contrasted against the gray stone walls gives a majestic color effect.

The Renaissance church was crowned by a cupola, square on plan, pillars, and a barrel vault or horizontal coffered ceiling. On the exterior were columns, pediments, and niches. Color and painted decoration as well as sculpture were subordinate to structural proportions in the best Renaissance church architecture.

Eventually the Renaissance gave place to the over-decoration of the Baroque, and it was probably partly as a protest against the gilt and polychrome of the Roman Catholic church of this period that the Protestant church went into the stark simplicity of puritanism of service and church decoration.

The New England white church is a result of simplicity of faith and living, but when we strive for simplicity in our churches today we should reappraise the architecture of the New England church. To be sure, it was a plain white church both on the exterior and in the interior, but its plainness was based on good proportion and honest materials. Also a factor which is often overlooked is the richness of detail. Heavy mouldings, architraves, panelling, pediments over doors and windows, and other finely proportioned architectural details add surface enrichment and even a feeling of color in the play of light and shade. The pattern of the small paned windows and the contrast of the dark pews, pulpit, and railings gives a feeling of color that is not present in a modern church with plain bleached pews and woodwork.

In contrast to the clean New England churches,

Church of the Resurrection, St. Louis, Missouri. Mural by Robert Harmon and Emil Frei. Sculpture by Hillis Arnold. Murphy and Mackey, architects.

the nineteenth-century Victorian churches of Gothic and Romanesque revival architecture had color, but it was drab and dirty-olive-green and schoolhouse-tan—and where there was color in the stained glass windows it was, for the most part, garish. In both subject matter and color, these windows were closely related to the chromo pictures so popular at the time.

Any present-day church with such nineteenth-century sentimental stained glass windows should send them to the scrap heap. But the present-day church also needs to be careful not to err on the side of monotony in the choice of a new color scheme. Indeed, many modern architects and decorators in their efforts to simplify and functionalize the present-day church produce a monotonous, neutral interior. Whether a new church is being built or an old church rebuilt and pulled out of the doldrums, great care must be taken lest we build a cold funeral-parlor-church with its cross cut out of the same material as the pews.

The church today as, in past ages, needs the beauty of color and the enrichment of ornament. However, present-day building costs demand substitutes for costly mosaics such as those in St. Bartholomew's Church and Christ Church Methodist, New York City. There must also be substitutes for costly imported stained glass windows. Temple Emanuel, San Francisco, California, combines vast expanses of white wall with accents of tile and marble. Plain white stucco walls may also be relieved by a wooden raftered ceiling. This may be left plain or decorated in colors. A wall of irregular panes of modern stained glass arranged in pattern may take the place of a traditional stained glass window and will admit a soft glow of light changing from dawn to dusk.

Color can often remedy interior decorative faults which are not structural in character. Even subdued color, in the hands of an expert, can give a sense of glow and splendor. The right use of color leads the mind away from dullness and fatigue. Also, when the mind is apt to wander in the midst of the service, it is best to have an object with beautiful color or even the beauty of flowers in the altar vases to draw the attention, rather than the hat on the woman in the pew ahead. Even a church flag or the Stars and Stripes will relieve the dead white of the New England church, or the stilted too-new church interior.

Color for church decoration requires careful study because of the physical, psychological, symbolical, and liturgical needs involved. First of all we need to know and understand the physical properties of color and color theory. We need to know what we can do with color, and what color can do for us.

Color may be reduced to three simple elements: *hue*—as yellow, red; *value*—as dark yellow, light red; and *intensity* (or brightness to grayness)—as intense yellow, dull red.

Although science has disproved the theory of red, blue, and yellow as the primary color impressions, this old theory of pigment primaries is the clearest way of teaching color to the uninitiated since it adjusts itself to a simple diagram or chart. If we draw a triangle and place red, blue, and yellow at opposite angles we have our primary triangle. Then if we superimpose a second triangle between the sides of the primary triangle its dotted line form will show the secondary colors which are made by a mixture of the first two colors on each side of the triangle. Thus yellow and blue make green, blue and red make violet, and red and yellow make orange if mixed together. Then if we draw lines from the apex of each triangle to the apex of the other triangle we will have our sets of complementary colors. Two complementary colors used in decoration form an opposing color harmony. Two complementaries mixed together in paint make a neutral gray. Notice the color triangles again and you will see that on one side you have blues and greens which are known as cool or receding or quiet colors. On the other side of the triangle are red, orange, and yellow which are the warm or advancing colors. Violet is a neutral, as is yellow or gold used in decoration.

Many mixtures of colors in between these primary hues are possible and these together with the grayed colors are most useful in decoration. Some of these grays are:

Slate (a mixture of violet and green)
Citrine (a mixture of green and orange)
Russet (a mixture of orange and violet)

Sage green (a mixture of green and slate)
Plum (a mixture of russet and slate)
Buff (a mixture of citrine and russet)

Gray may be a mixture of any two primaries and will take on the character of the one most in quantity. Gray should always have color character and not be dead black and white. It is also possible for black to vary. The strongest hues and colors of brightest intensity should be used for accents and the grayer tones for large areas. Thus the walls, floors, and even the upholstery on pews should be subdued in tone, while colors about the altar may be stronger in hue.

As we have stated, color schemes or color harmonies can be made up of opposing or complementary colors. When complementary colors are placed side by side they intensify each other. However, near complementaries such as blue and orange-yellow instead of orange, or red and green-blue instead of green are finer harmonies than the exact complementary. When the surface of both colors is broken, we get a reduced contrast. Also a large quantity of one color and a small amount of its complementary produces a different effect.

Another type of color harmony is composed of related colors such as blue and green; or yellow, orange, and tan. Such color schemes are used by modern decorators and are easier to work with than complementary color schemes.

The simple harmonies of related color may seem too simple, but when relieved by texture, as in hand-woven materials, or by interesting wall surfaces, give an effect of richness. The blue of the sky varying from light to dark and from green-blue to even ultramarine is an example of a related harmony in nature. Large masses of foliage varying from yellow-green to blue-green give a related color scheme, and the autumn landscape provides a color scheme of yellow, orange, and orange-red and even the low-key tones of dried grasses.

Color schemes may also consist of the three primary colors, red, blue, and yellow. This type of color scheme is found in primitive art and also in many religious paintings of the old masters.

When using colors, we have to consider value and intensity as well as hue. A bright intensity or a dark value of certain colors may not be pleasing while a less intense value of the same color might be pleasing. It is often necessary to reduce the tone or intensity contrasts of colors in order to get a satisfactory harmony, since sharp contrasts of pure color sometimes change the colors themselves. Unless a startling effect is desired, the tone

Alpine Community Church, Alpine, California. The altar, cross, and reredos panels are of colorful vitreous enamel on copper. Church symbols are worked into contemporary designs of blue, gold, green, and brick red. The chancel wall is brick. Enamels by Margaret Montgomery.

contrasts of large masses of color should be slight. However, small quantities of color with sharp tone contrasts can be pleasing, as seen in the brilliant vibration of light and dark colors in a primitive woven textile.

To harmonize colors that clash badly:

1—Mix a little of each color with the other. If you cannot actually mix the colors you can make a stipple of each over the surface of the other.

2—Mix a third color or stipple it over each of the other colors.

3—Use an outline of dark or light around the colors. A broad outline of light or dark will bring out the brilliance of the colors.

We also need to consider the space to be covered and the quantity of the color to be used. Large masses of color placed side by side appear altogether different from the same colors arranged in small quantities. Colors arranged in stripes appear different from the same colors in an all-over pattern. By changing the texture of the surface, a color effect can be changed. Position in the room also determines the use of color. Thus brilliant hues may be used to decorate the wooden beams of a church, while the same colors used on the reredos in the well-lighted chancel would seem harsh.

Church decoration requires a careful use of color and presents some problems that do not arise when using color in the decoration of a private dwelling or an auditorium. The color scheme of a church must be pleasing and it must have warmth, but it must never be garish or pretty, nor should it reflect the current decorating fads. Greens should be avoided in the chancel as should large quantities of other cold or retreating colors. A warm color will help to connect the chancel with the nave.

A dark church, a light church, a traditional church, or a modern church all present different problems of color decoration. A dark church—and to a certain extent all churches are dark compared to the average living room—requires strong, bright color, at least for accents. There should be sufficient contrast of tone or intensity to light up the darkness. Strong red, blue, green, white, and yellow are beautiful in semi-darkness. In the church, we may have bright colors combined with gold on the ceilings, which are usually in shadow, and on the chancel below a window; and the cool tints of blue, green, or white may be on the side walls.

A decorative design for a chapel chancel might be in rose, flame color, gold, and white upon a background of lustrous blue. Not only should the color be of sufficient brightness, but the design should be simple and the shapes large enough to count without clashing with the windows. The same type of color, but of less intensity, could be used on the lighter walls of the nave, which are nearer to the eye.

Egyptian and Pompeian wall decorations are examples of color designed for dark situations. The reflected light subdued their brightness. In a direct light, these decorations appear garish. Again the wall space between windows is dark, and if decoration is put on this space the colors may be strong if they are tone contrasts.

Many church windows are chosen without regard to the color scheme of the church and, when placed, jar with the colors of walls and other furnishings. Stained glass seems to go with Gothic oak beams and dark wooden pews, and when in doing over an old church we bleach the woodwork we may destroy the feeling of support needed for the colored glass.

Color applied to a wall takes away its rigidity. It can change the dimensions and placement of a wall. It can shorten or lengthen distances, raise or lower a ceiling, light or darken a room, thicken or eliminate a wall, and change the atmosphere of a room. Thus warm colors make the wall seem nearer and cool colors make it recede. Pale shades on walls make the walls more distant, and strong hues bring the walls nearer and make the room smaller. A light color stresses the weight and solidity of the wall. The texture of a wall makes the wall heavy and near, or smooth and far. A brilliant shiny surface seems nearer. Color can enhance the volume of a building and change its general exterior aspect. The interior color scheme of a building can be in keeping and related to the purpose of each room.

Neutral tones such as tans and grays have little effect on architectural space. Light colors en-

St. Stephen's Episcopal Church, Columbus, Ohio. Clerestory light falls upon the tall Plexiglas cross above the altar. The cross was designed by Laura Ziegler and is formed of steel with plastic inserts of reds and blue-greens. Theodore Brooks and Gilbert Coddington, architects.

hance, but strong primary colors can destroy the unity of a surface and should thus be used only as accents.

The value, or darkness or lightness of a color, is important in church decoration. When placing an object such as a cross, it is well to know that a light object increases its size against a dark background, while a dark object seems smaller against a light ground because of irradiation. Intensity of color is also important. Usually, the less intense or gray tones are used for large areas such as walls, with the intense color for accent.

Color in church decoration should enhance the architecture and structure of the building. A color scheme should be in harmony with the wood and stone. There is no material in architecture that does not have color. We can ignore the colors of marble, brick, terra cotta, stone, or cement, but the best decoration uses these structural colors as a part of the color scheme. There is warm sandstone, gray stone, and stone of pale pink tones. We have many different colors in brick, and there are marbles of all colors. In the wooden church, we have the choice of warm redwood, yellow pine, and the browns of walnut and mahogany. All these materials should be considered in the planning of the color scheme.

Both a good and a bad example of harmony between decoration and architectural background are found in a well-known New York church. The old sandstone Gothic arches are a lovely purplish red, and the material on the pew cushions matches the sandstone to good effect. However, the red dossal behind the chapel altar, which is visible to all in the church, is a discordant shade of red and does not harmonize with the mural which is the chief decoration of the church.

Color should not destroy form, but emphasize it and also enhance the native qualities of the raw materials. The church of modern architecture needs color to relieve its plainness, while a church with much carving and sculpture will require less color in its background spaces.

The amount of color used is important since the total effect of a color scheme depends not only upon the properties of each color, but upon the proportion used. Thus a pleasant balance of color is established with a large space of cool color and a smaller one of warm color, whereas if the spaces were reversed, with the large space of warm color, you would get a disquieting effect.

Color schemes are affected by conditions of light, both natural and artificial, and for this reason color schemes should be planned on the spot and should be tested in all variations of light. A gray day, a cloudy sky, dazzling sunlight, and pale sunlight all affect color differently. Intense sunshine will reduce color which has no depth and will add a yellow tint to all colors so that strong orange and green will be more harmonious under yellow light. Black loses its somberness in sunlight. Gray light is better for medium strength colors and broken tints, while darkness calls for strong color. Color schemes also change in artificial light and colors which appear harmonious in shadow will jump at one when the electric lights are turned on. Blues and greens seem darker in artificial light and lose much of their color character. If you use fluorescent lighting, you have another color problem. Blues and greens seem yellowish and faded. Pink and rose seem yellowish, and deep yellow takes on a reddish tint. Peach and cream are normal good shades in fluorescent light, and the tans seem yellowish, while deep blues are so grayed that they lose color. One can well see how fluorescent lighting would completely ruin a decorative scheme planned for ordinary light. Also, the filtered light that comes through stained glass windows can cause drastic changes in the colors of walls, carpets, hangings, and even wood colors.

Each color has its own characteristics and its psychological and symbolical effects and meanings, and if we understand these properties of colors we can use them more intelligently.

Green is a cool, retiring color. It is the color most seen in nature, though this is not a fixed green but a pulsing variety of greens. Green light is the brightest light, and pure green preserves its visibility longest in twilight. However, green is a hard color to use in decoration and should be used in moderation along with yellow, orange, or rose. Green is at its loveliest in silk and in green porcelain. Green in its soft tones is good for rugs, but a large green carpet is a mistake as it does not seem to support the furniture or give a firm footing. Green walls above a dark panelling of wood are excellent, and dark wood furniture looks well upholstered in green, for green needs the support and restraining enclosure of dark wood. Psychologically, green is the expression of quiet and hope and victory. It is the color of spring and therefore a pleasant color.

Red is a warm, advancing color. Red signifies fire, divine love, creative power, and royalty. In a bad sense, red signifies horror, blood, and war. The Roman Catholic Church uses red and knows its impressiveness. We have red robes, red uni-

forms, and red carpets to quicken the pulse on special occasions.

Red in decoration is a good color for a carpet, a rug, or a redstone floor. Red is good for seating, such as pew cushions. On the walls, red makes the rooms smaller as it advances to meet the eye. Red is beautiful in glass, in silk, and in woolen materials, but red velvet suggests the theatrical. Red is beautiful with a gray or a black setting or balanced by white as in Japanese art. One should also study the Renaissance painters for the use of red.

Blue is cool and receding. It suggests repose. Blue is so deficient in light that it does not carry at a distance. Silver and gold give blue a luminous effect. Blue suggests heaven, truth, fidelity, and is the color of the Virgin. Blue is best when suspended and is thus good on walls or for draperies. Blue when used horizontally catches too much light and thus seems colorless. Blue is excellent in glass and in pottery and tilework. Too much blue is depressing.

Yellow is the lightest color. It is the symbol of

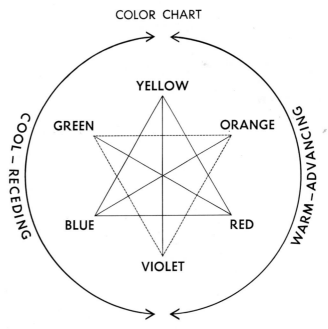

COLOR CHART

Primary Colors: Blue, Red, Yellow
Secondary Colors: Orange, Violet, Green
Complementary Colors:
Blue & Orange, Red & Green, Violet & Yellow

57

Church of St. Columba, Chester, New York. This colorful mural of tempera on concrete block gives distinction to the otherwise simple wood construction of the church. Wilhelm Wagner, artist.

the sun, of the goodness of God. Yellow is cheerful and light. It is a good background for all colors. We see it as the background for mosaics and on the gold baroque reredos of Mexican churches. It is beautiful in silk, velvet, and brocade. It is beautiful on walls or for upholstery. Gold is always good for framing, and gold and silver and gold and white are harmonious. If used in strongly lighted rooms, the quieter shades of yellow, such as buff and tan, are best, but beware of a dull mustard color that absorbs all light. Tones of yellow go well with the walnut, mahogany, and golden or dark oak. Brown, which is a derivative of yellow, is good for draperies or upholstery, but should be used in small quantities since it makes for dullness and darkness.

Violet may partake of the qualities of blue or red. Violet becomes blue in twilight so that violet materials are dependent on lighting. Blue-violet hangs better than red-violet and is thus more suitable for curtains or dossals. Red-violet is better for carpeting and for upholstery. Violet is harmonized by brown and thus usable where there is wood panelling or dark pews. It is also good with gold and silver. Violet is pleasing in silk, velvet, and wool. Violet in too great quantity produces sadness.

Grays are excellent backgrounds. Gray dissolves colors while brown emphasizes colors. Gray has a light effect and is not as good for upholstery or carpet as brown. Gray is suitable for hangings and for walls because of its light effect. Silver is a gleaming gray, and gives a harmonious effect, especially to cool colors such as blue and green.

Through the ages certain colors have become associated with the saints, evangelists, and other characters in religious art. These colors were used in a symbolical or mystic sense. This use of color was scrupulously followed in old stained glass and in early painting. The colors in which the evangelists were usually represented are as follows:

St. Matthew	green
St. Mark	purple
St. Luke	blue
St. John	rosy red

The colors for the apostles and saints are:

St. James the Great	green
St. James the Less	brown
St. Thomas	gray
St. Mary	blue
St. Peter	deep blue
St. Agnes	green and white
St. Matthias	murrey or brick-red
St. Bartholomew	purple-brown
St. Jude	tan
St. Andrew	red
St. Simon	green-blue
St. Philip	red
St. George	red and white
St. Nicholas	heather purple
St. Paul	purple and white
St. Patrick	green and gold

These symbolical colors might be used to form the basis of a color scheme to decorate a chapel dedicated to a particular apostle or saint.

In decorating an Episcopal, Lutheran, or Roman Catholic church we need to know the liturgical colors used, because these colors will be in constant use on the altars and in the vestments of the priests or ministers.

Any colors used in the church decorations should be in harmony with the liturgical colors. In the Middle Ages the use of color varied and each cathedral had its own use. Today we use the Western use and that of Salisbury Cathedral (Sarum). The Sarum use is as follows:

Best—Christmas, Epiphany, Easter, Ascension, Whitsunday, Trinity, Dedication, Patronal Festival, All Saints', Thanksgiving.

Second Best—Weekdays in Epiphanytide and Trinitytide (if red not used).

Red—In Octave of Epiphany, Sundays after Epiphany, Septuagesima through Ash Wednesday, Passiontide to Easter Eve, Sundays after Trinity, Holy Innocents, Apostles, Martyrs, and Evangelists (except St. John), Baptisms, Confirmation.

White—St. John the Evangelist, during Octave of Christmas, Circumcision, Eastertide, Rogation Days, Friday and Saturday before Whitsunday, during Octave of Trinity, the Transfiguration, Feasts of the B.V.M., Saints' days in Eastertide, Virgins, Michaelmas.

Blue—Advent and as alternate color for the following: Pre-Lenten season, Nativity of St. John Baptist, All Souls' Day, Funerals, Requiems.

Black—All Souls' Day, Funerals, Requiems.

Unbleached linen—Days of Lent until Passion Sunday.

The Lutheran rules are strict and clear. The altar, vestments, hangings, pulpit and lectern falls are the day or the season irrespective of the service involved. The color use is:

White—Christmas Eve through Epiphanytide; Easter Day to Whitsun Eve; The Transfiguration and Sunday near it; Feasts of Apostles (except St. John) and of Martyrs; All Saints'; Dedication of a Church; Church Anniversaries; Harvest Festival and Thanksgiving.

Green—First Vespers of Septuagesima through Shrove Tuesday; II Trinity through to the First Vespers of I Advent.

Violet—First Vespers of I Advent to Christmas Eve; Vespers of Shrove Tuesday through to Vespers of Easter Eve (except Good Friday).

Black—Good Friday, and a Day of Humiliation.

The Western Use of color is:

White—Christmas and days of Octave; Circumcision; Epiphany and Octave; Maundy Thursday; Easter Even through the Fifth Sunday after Easter; Ascension Eve through Vigil of Pentecost; Trinity Sunday; Corpus Christi and Octave; Transfiguration; Christ the King; Feasts of the B.V.M.; All Saints' and Octave; Michaelmas; Confessors, Doctors, Virgins, and Holy Women.

Red—Pentecost and Octave; Apostles and Evangelists (except St. John, white); Martyrs (Holy Innocents if on Sunday).

Violet—Advent Season, except third Sunday, Gaudete; Septuagesima through to Maundy Thursday, except Fourth Sunday in Lent, Laetare; Ember Days except those in Octave of Pentecost; Rogation Days; Vigils; Holy Innocents, if not on a Sunday.

Green—The Sundays (and Ferias) after the Octave of Epiphany through to the Eve of Septuagesima; the Sundays (and Ferias) after Pentecost (or after Trinity) through to Advent.

Black—Good Friday; All Souls'; Requiem.

Rose—Third Sunday in Advent (Gaudete); Fourth Sunday in Lent (Laetare).

An outstanding example of the modern use of color and light is being carried out in the new Coventry Cathedral in Coventry, England. On either side of the cathedral are to be pairs of stained glass windows of abstract design set in saw-toothed recessions in the walls. The windows face toward the altar rather than facing one another. The pair nearest the church entrance is predominantly green to suggest man's youth; the next pair, red for maturity; the next, multicolor for middle age; the fourth pair, in blues and purples for old age; and the last pair nearest the altar, orange and yellows symbolic of after life. The designs of the windows are symbolic and contain such objects as the chalice, the seven-branched candelabra, hands, stars, and the all-seeing eye. The emotional effect sought is that of a fusion of architecture and glass so that one feels as if one has entered another world.

A similar progression of color is noted in the stained glass windows in the Washington Memorial Chapel at Valley Forge, Pennsylvania. The windows at the back and sides of the nave are blue and purple, while the predominant colors in the chancel windows are reds and oranges.

In redecorating a church, color should be used to emphasize and articulate the architecture—in a Gothic church the vaulting and ribs. Such a redecorating job was done in Broadway Congregational Church by Rambusch, Inc. under the supervision of Adams & Woodbridge, architects. The architectural features were painted limestone gray with green vaulting ribs and rosy tan walls to give a feeling of warmth to the nave. The rosy tan also made a flattering background for the occupants of the nave. The same principle of color scheme could be used in the church of classic architecture.

A small Gothic chapel which had green nave walls, rust color chancel walls, and a madonna window of blue and green stained glass was redecorated. The nave was painted dusty rose and the chancel walls azure blue which made a beautiful setting for the window.

When the chancel walls are dark in tone, the altar must be rich in decoration or color so that

Zion Evangelical Lutheran Church, Kalamazoo, Michigan. The large stained glass window which dominates the eastern wall makes an impressive setting for the simple altar of oak and brick. The predominant colors of the window are red and blue, which add warmth and richness to the dignity of the beautiful proportions of the church. The planting below the chancel is one of the few installations of permanent plant material that we have seen that seems to belong as a part of the design. Charles Edward Slade & Associates, architects.

it stands out in glory.

Here are some typical problems of redecorating:

Question: We have a Gothic church with a dark stained ceiling. What colors shall we use in redecorating?

Answer: Keep the dark ceiling as that is suitable for Gothic architecture.

Paint the walls warm gray. Upholster the pews in the same color. Paint the chancel walls dull vermilion. Carpet the aisles in deep dull vermilion (terra cotta) carpet.

Question: Our church has dark panelled oak walls. The aisles are tiled with a pattern of brick red, green, and blue tiles and the reredos is gold. What can we do to lighten and improve it?

Answer: Refinish the panelling in a waxed natural brown tone—not too light or it will not seem to support the stained glass windows.

Paint your nave walls dull marigold yellow with the chancel wall blue-green as a setting for the gold and polychrome reredos. Upholster the pews in dark reddish brown to match the panelling.

Question: We have a large stained glass window with blues, gold, and orange colorings. What colors can we use to redecorate the church?

Answer: Paint the walls of the chancel where the window is dull vermilion. Paint the nave walls the same color but several shades lighter. Upholster the pews in dark vermilion. Carpet the aisles in dull gold.

Question: We have a chapel with a beautiful stained glass reredos. The walls are tan with a gold stencil design and the ceiling is of wooden rafters with polychrome decoration. There is gray stonework and gray flagstone aisles. We like the decoration as it is, but the walls are dirty, and it is too expensive to redecorate them with the gold leaf stencil. What would you suggest? The pew cushions are now red.

Answer: Do the chancel walls over using the gold stencil against a blue-green or dull vermilion painted ground. Paint the nave walls deep ivory or very pale vermilion without any stencil. The added color on the chancel walls will give emphasis to the altar and the plain nave walls will

keep their place. Upholster the pew cushions in warm tan.

Question: Our church is New England style. It needs redecorating. What colors would you suggest?

Answer: Paint the walls platinum gray. At the windows, hang draperies of same gray color with a gold thread in weave. Upholster the pews in gold and put a gold carpet on the center aisle. Black asphalt tile could also be used on the old floor or if good enough it can be refinished and left uncovered.

Architect's drawing of St. Martha's Mission, West Covina, California. Carleton Winslow, architect.

7

Church Furniture

IN the ancient church, seats were not necessary since the posture of worship was chiefly kneeling or standing. For the aged, stone seats were provided against the walls. These seats formed a part of the structure of the walls. Seats were also built around the base of pillars and against the nave and chancel walls. From the earliest times, stalls and fixed seats were provided in the chancel for the priests. The sedilia, or group of three graduating seats, were built into the stone walls. Later, heavy stone seats and plain wooden stalls were built. In Gothic times, these stalls were richly carved with pinnacled canopies. Misericords, or hinged seats which could be turned up, were also used in the chancel.

Fixed seats in the nave of the church were not introduced until the fourteenth century. The first seats were plain massive benches with heavy mouldings. By the fifteenth century, pews with elaborate carving were used. These benches or pews had ends carved with symbolic ornament or Gothic tracery. The ends were square-headed or "poppy topped," that is, topped with a heavy carved finial in the shape of a fleur-de-lis and with human or beast-head figure carvings. Some of the finest Gothic carving was done on these fifteenth- and sixteenth-century bench ends.

Parcloses, or private pews, were placed at the front end of the aisles. These were for royalty, titled persons, and lords of the manor. Private pews increased in number during the Reformation. These pews had seats on all sides and were made to face the pulpit rather than the altar. The sides were high for warmth and also to keep the occupants from being seen so that they would not need to bow to the Gloria. The seats were upholstered, and often separate chairs and sofas were installed and even fireplaces and canopies built, and there were doors with locks.

The manor pew became the family pew of the eighteenth century. These family pews can be seen in many old churches in both England and America today. The position of the family pew was dictated by the importance of the families or their connection with the church. Those who held such offices as church wardens or vestrymen had pews near the font. The pews were usually floored with wood and raised one step above the floor of the aisles. This custom of raising church pews a step from the aisle and having locked doors continued down into the nineteenth century and many are in use in churches today, particularly in the old churches of New York, Philadelphia, and other east coast cities. Long after the rectangular family cubicle pews disappeared, the church pew continued to have a latched door at either aisle.

The church aisles as we see them today were the innovation of Sir Christopher Wren. Wren's ideal plan for church seating included benches with wide alleys which provided the extra beauty of the open space, a feature to be considered in the seating arrangements of the modern church.

A seating plan is essential for the present-day church not only to secure the best arrangement of pews, but also to give the greatest possible seating capacity in a given space. Although it means less seating space, a wide central aisle will add to the architectural dignity of the church. The architect should furnish the seating plan, but when new pews are being ordered without consultation with an architect, there are several church furniture companies that will advise on seating problems and even furnish a seating plan to fit individual church requirements.

In planning the seating of a church you must consider all exits, radiators, columns or posts, wall offsets, and other obstructions. The space required in front of the pulpit and the passage space

St. Andrew's Lutheran Church, Park Ridge, Illinois. A twenty-one-foot carved oak cross hangs above a large altar of brick and stone with carved oak plaque insets. The brick wall of the chancel is fluted, as is the form of the pulpit and the lectern. Charles Edward Slade & Associates, architects.

at the rear must be defined, and the number and width of the aisles must be determined.

There are three types of seating plans most generally used in churches today. The plan most satisfactory from the standpoint of architectural balance is the plan with the wide center aisle and a group of pews on each side of the aisle. This type of pew arrangement is especially desirable in Episcopal and Lutheran churches, because of the procession. The minimum width for this center aisle is 5 feet 6 inches. The side aisles should have a minimum width of 4 feet.

Another plan for arranging church pews is with a center aisle and two side aisles, with pews to the side of each side aisle. This plan is suitable for a wide church. When the pews are served by five aisles instead of the customary three, the arrangement divides the pews into smaller units and avoids the discomfort of passing many persons in order to reach the inside seats. If a church does not require the wide center aisle for the procession, it is possible to get greater seating capacity when pews are placed in the center space of the nave with two side aisles, with pews also at the side of the side aisles.

Of course the plan for the pew arrangement is indicated by the size and proportions of the nave and by the location of the doorways.

It is recommended that the minimum spacing between pews in a church requiring kneeling facilities be 3 feet back to back where possible. One thing to remember is to allow plenty of space under the seat itself for the feet of the worshipper when kneeling. The height, slope, and depth of the seat, and the slope and height of the seat back are important. In most present-day pews, both the seat and back are shaped to give natural support and the curves follow the curves of the body. Seats and backs are placed at proper angles for correct posture and restful comfort. Backs of pews usually range from 19½ inches in height to 21 inches and from 15 to 16 inches in width. An incline of 5½ inches is satisfactory. Eighteen inches should be allowed for each person.

Most pews are built of oak and can be obtained in several finishes—light, dark, or silver. Pews are also available in mahogany and other hard woods, such as birch, elm, poplar, yellow pine, and red gum. Walnut and mahogany are more expensive than the other woods mentioned. Pew ends are

Bertha E. R. Strosacker Memorial Presbyterian Church, Midland, Michigan. The lighting fixtures are made of four-foot and two-foot fluorescent lamps mounted on a silver framework with crystal pendant drops. The floors are carpeted. Edward Coe Embury and Aymar Embury II, architects.

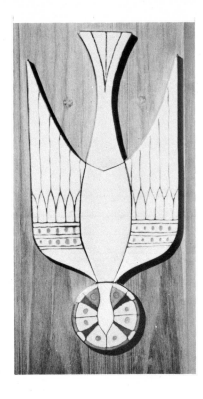

Enamel decoration on baptismal font at Pacific School of Religion, Berkeley, California. Designed by Margaret Montgomery.

available in many stock designs, including square and shaped with squared, curved, or pointed tops. There are plain pew ends, pew ends with a variety of mouldings, and wainscoted and carved pew ends. Painted pews in colonial panelled designs are also available.

Many stock pews are decorated with carved crosses, of various types within or without a surrounding circle, rectangle, or diamond. Other pews carved with more elaborate symbols and Gothic tracery are also available. However, the plainer the design of the pew ends and the better the wood, construction, and workmanship of the pew, the more satisfactory it will be.

Of course pews may be custom built at a factory or you may have the local carpenter build your pews. However, if you choose a simple well-built stock pattern, you can usually get a satisfactory pew.

Often a church—even a new church—is enhanced by retaining its old pews, if these pews are of hard wood and good workmanship and not too uncomfortable. Old pews will give a mellow note where everything else seems too new.

The pews of the church are there for one pur-

pose only and that is to seat the congregation. Pews should be as inconspicuous as possible as they should not detract from the service or from the general effect of the architecture. If the pews are to have cushions, the upholstery should be durable and usually of a neutral background color. More information about upholstery materials for pews will be given in another chapter.

Pews may be had with folding kneelers attached to their backs, for churches that prefer this type of kneeler to the individual hassock or kneeling pad.

The use of individual opera seats in churches is to be regretted since they give an unpleasant appearance and destroy the dignity and religious tone of the church. Chapel chairs with rush bottoms, which are used in many suburban and country churches and chapels, are attractive in appearance and have the advantage of giving each person an individual seat. Chapel chairs have so small a scale that their use appears to increase the spatial qualities of a small room. Such chairs can be lashed together in rows to avoid the problem of having to realign them constantly.

When buying pews, it is optional to have the assembling and installation included in the contract price. However, it is possible to buy semi-assembled pews and have the assembling and installation done by a carpenter or maintenance man. When ordering pews it is necessary to state the kind of floor, that is, the material of which the floor is made, such as wood, concrete, or tile. Also it is necessary to state whether the floor is level or on a slant, or possibly bowl-shaped and slanting from three directions.

Among other items of church furniture that are available from many manufacturers are wooden pulpits, lecterns, prayer desks, clergy chairs, and baptismal fonts. With good taste as your guide it is possible to select such items of church furniture from stock patterns. However, there are so many poor designs among the few that are in good simple proportions that one has to be very discriminating. Unless the church has money to have a good artist design such furniture to order, it is always best to select the simplest design available and pay for good construction rather than second-rate decoration.

The pulpit is usually the same height as the lectern, plus steps. There may be as many steps as desirable according to the proportions of the nave and the size of the pulpit itself. The position of the pulpit has changed through the ages. At the present time the pulpit in the church liturgical plan is placed in the nave at one side of the chancel, with the lectern on the other side. There are still many churches with the pulpit in the center of the platform and, of course, the Christian Science church has two pulpits. The pulpit should be of good wood and sturdy workmanship, or it may be of stone to harmonize with the church walls. The pulpit may also be of metal. If extra money is available, a pulpit may be designed to order and embellished with appropriate carving or other decoration.

In churches of liturgical design, the lectern is second in importance to the pulpit and is placed on the opposite side of the chancel. In design it should harmonize with the pulpit. The lectern is usually smaller than the pulpit and needs a doorway or some other architectural feature to help balance the pulpit. The lectern is often hung with a silk hanging which changes color with the church season, and this hanging gives added emphasis to the lectern.

The lectern may be of iron, brass, or bronze, instead of wood, and of course it may be built of stone or marble or other material and be a part of the architecture of the church. The desk-shaped lectern upon a pedestal with a rack for the Bible, or a carved eagle holding the Bible, is

Enamel decoration on pulpit at Pacific School of Religion, Berkeley, California. Designed by Margaret Montgomery.

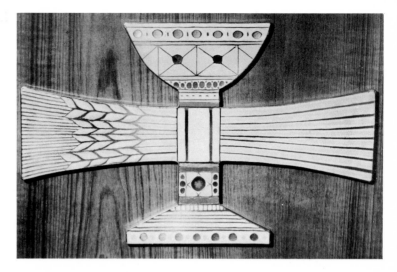

Colored enamel decoration on copper, for wood altar, at Pacific School of Religion, Berkeley, California. Designed by Margaret Montgomery.

the traditional lectern design, but a simple tall rectangular desk may be used. The lectern is usually about 45 inches in height to be convenient to the reader. It should be from 20 to 28 inches in width and from 17 to 20 inches in depth in order to accommodate a Bible of good size.

If you are building a church of Gothic or Colonial design, or refurnishing such a church, it is possible to get stock pulpits and other furniture suitable and harmonious with the architecture. It is even possible to order an altar complete with its own reredos and chancel panelling. You can buy "chancel sets" with matching altar, pulpit, lectern, baptismal font, pulpit chair, and flower stands (altar interchangeable with a communion table according to the denomination). Or you may order a matched pulpit set with a "neatly carved" pulpit, pulpit chair, side pulpit chairs, communion table, two communion chairs and two flower stands!!

The chairs, communion table, and other moveable furniture used in the church should be made in a style that harmonizes with the architecture. The wood should be the same as the church woodwork, when it is natural wood. Most stock furniture for churches is too heavy, and in design it is either Gothic or Mission. It is often, to say the least, ugly and poorly designed.

If there ever was any good reason why church

furniture should be made Mission style, with a bit of Gothic chiseling, it has long outlived that reason.

As the design of the present-day church building takes on new dimensions, so do, or should, the furniture and other fittings. The pulpit, lectern, and other articles of church furniture that have followed traditional styles for so many centuries must now change their style and dimensions in order to harmonize with the modern church. Thus we find pulpits built of brick to match the brick walls, or of aluminum, in a modern design to harmonize with the aluminum cross over the altar. Marble pulpits in new open work designs are also a new venture in church design. Indeed, the revolution in church architecture calls for a change in every article designed for the church.

In the sanctuary of St. Scholastic, Aspinwall, Pittsburgh, Pennsylvania, the seats for the priests are round stools of modern design which stand unobtrusively against the wall. The altar is red granite against a gray plaster reredos wall, with side walls of fieldstone against which stand two modern limestone statues on limestone bases. As you can see, no traditional designs of church chairs could conceivably be used in this setting.

Architect's drawing of First Presbyterian Church, Elkhart, Indiana.
Harold E. Wagoner—Wiley & Miller Associates, architects.

8

Lighting for Churches

DEVOTIONAL lights were placed before the altar before the thirteenth century, and by the thirteenth century, candles were used on the altar and were carried in procession. Special lights were used at Christmas, Candlemas, and Easter. At Christmas they were carried by everyone in the procession. These lights were cresset cups fastened to poles. Cresset cups and mortars holding oil and a wick were also placed in the chancel and at doorways. Brackets with prickets for candles date from medieval times and candelabra made of latten, an amalgam of brass, date from the fourteenth century. These candelabra were usually designed with a central figure of the Virgin and two tiers of branches with sockets for candles. In the seventeenth and eighteenth centuries, candelabra were generally made of brass. There were also wrought iron corona lights holding a crown of candles, which hung before the rood screen.

There are no traditions in church illumination except for the devotional lights used in the sanctuary and in processions. However, by the seventeenth and eighteenth centuries the general illumination of churches was by means of brass candelabra, sometimes designed to hold as many as a hundred candles. Examples of eighteenth-century brass candelabra, or branches, are found in several early American churches, notably St. Michael's, Charlestown, North Carolina, Christ Church, Philadelphia, and Trinity Church, Newport, Rhode Island. St. Paul's Chapel, New York City, has fourteen magnificent original Waterford glass candelabra which hang from a ceiling of cerulean blue.

It was almost the middle of the nineteenth century when gas light was first used. As of necessity, gas and candle fixtures pointed upward, and the first electric fixtures followed this design.

Many of these old fixtures are still in use, since the first electric lamp was made not more than seventy-five years ago. The science of lighting has developed rapidly, but it is only within the last few years, since the development of high wattage lamps, that new developments in lighting have been applied to the design and execution of suitable illumination equipment for church interiors.

Churches present unique problems of lighting. Most churches are under-lighted or over-lighted. Either of these extremes can destroy the effectiveness of the architecture and the beauty of the decorations. Too much light of the wrong kind can change colors and cause glare that will irritate the nerves and destroy the atmosphere of the service. Too little light can cast unpleasant shadows and gloom, and also make it impossible to use prayer book, missal, or hymnal.

The proper church illumination should enhance the beauty of the architecture and decorations as well as preserve the spiritual values of the ecclesiastical atmosphere. The problems of church illumination are too involved for the inexperienced. Nor can the lighting of a church be satisfactorily handled by the architect or decorator alone. In the long run, the most satisfactory plan is to get an experienced lighting consultant. If the project is a new church, the lighting consultant can plan the lighting together with the architect. If an old church needs re-lighting, a lighting consultant will survey the building and test the light intensities to find how far they come from meeting the I.E.S. standards for reading light for the nave, which is 10 foot-candles. He will also inspect the wiring and see that it meets the requirements of the National Board of Fire Underwriters and City Inspection Departments.

From the aesthetic standpoint, the lighting consultant can not only enhance the architectural

design by directing light and shadow where they should be, but he can correct architectural proportions that are not right. Thus a church that seems squatty because of a nave that is too short can be made to appear longer by the proper location of two rows of lanterns. A church which has an atmosphere of coldness may be given warmth and spiritual calmness by the use of amber lights directed so as to give extra light in the chancel and to give height and space. The correct use of light can take out spotty shadows that destroy carving and can preserve the true color of murals and other decorations. Artistic lighting can also be made to conform with and accentuate the different moods of the service.

In a new church, when the architect and the lighting consultant work together, light can become a part of the architectural plan.

In re-lighting an old church which was not originally designed for electric light, or at least not for the light needed today, the problem is more difficult. However, many lighting fixtures forty or fifty years old are of good design that harmonizes with the architecture. Although they may not give enough light, they are more suitable than new fixtures, and it is better to alter the old fixtures than to install new ones. When possible, it is less expensive to alter the old fixtures without taking them down.

The ideal plan of illumination for churches is to provide general illumination with types of fixtures that will give well-distributed, low-intensity, general lighting and with supplementary light for specific areas, such as the altar, pulpit, lectern, choir, and pews.

The first type of fixture that provides general illumination is the lantern. Lanterns were first used in the church with high wattage lamps and diffused glass, often colored, and these gave a quality of light related to the light that came from stained glass windows. With the increased use of churches at night and the necessary demands for light to read by, these diffused light lanterns no longer give a satisfactory light. In fact surveys

made with light meters show that the light from these lanterns is usually far below standards called for by the I.E.S.

However, the lantern gives a satisfactory architectural effect, since lanterns can be designed to harmonize with different styles of architecture. When lanterns are used it is the accepted practice to hang two rows aligned with the sanctuary or chancel arch. The best effect is obtained by suspending the lanterns at a point between the trusses of the architectural bays and in line with the windows. The number of lanterns will depend upon the number of architectural bays. The two rows of lanterns should never be placed closer than half the width of the church. The resulting two rows of lanterns, with uniform spacing, height, and brightness, create two lines of light that converge and induce attention toward the altar, where the service is taking place. Such architectural features as a balcony can change the placing of fixtures. Lanterns and other hanging fixtures must be designed to look well unlighted as well as lighted.

Lanterns of Gothic design are usually made of wrought iron. Brass or bronze lanterns are used in Romanesque and Renaissance churches, while Colonial fixtures can be of brass or crystal. Lanterns of modern design are made of all metals, including steel and aluminum. In order to increase the efficiency of present-day church lanterns, all glass is placed vertically so that a minimum of dust is collected. The design of lanterns is also controlled to include few horizontal lines that would obstruct the light. Pale amber bulb lamps and limited wattage are used to avoid excessive brightness. However, a standard lamp placed behind an amber diffusing panel gives the same effect at less replacement cost. The size of each lantern must be in scale with the area in which it is installed. Such large lanterns as those used in Radio City Music Hall would be too theatrical for a church.

Also, if the wattage of each lantern is too high, or the bulbs placed too low in the lantern, it will produce glare. A lantern with one bulb lamp and no bottom glass is most satisfactory from the standpoint of maintenance since it is easier to replace one bulb. Also one large bulb gives more

St. Paul's Chapel of Trinity Parish, New York City, built in 1766. Night lighting on beautiful old tower and porch columns of American Georgian architecture.

Temple Beth-El, Springfield, Massachusetts. Pillar of Fire by Ibram Lassaw. Welded bronze figure, twenty-eight feet high, eleven feet wide, and three feet deep, is set against the curved stone wall and is lighted at night by spotlights.

light and costs less than several small bulbs. The open-bottom lantern does not collect dirt and bugs and is therefore no cleaning problem. Lanterns with down lighting may be used in such areas as the choir. Lanterns are often wired for two or more circuits of light. When lanterns or other suspended fixtures are used, the sight lines of the congregation must be studied so that the fixture is placed at the right height.

Dome lighting in a suspended fixture with a silvered bowl lamp and a large diffusing bowl will give glareless down lighting. However, this is not completely satisfactory because it can only be used at certain heights. When a dome reflector is made of perforated metal, a combination of upward and down lighting can be obtained.

However, more general illumination is usually needed than can be obtained from a hanging fixture. Thus lanterns or dome lights should be supplemented by another form of illumination such as down lighting. This consists of fixtures with 100- to 1000-watt capacity which can be concealed in the ceiling and brought into use only

when the congregation needs to read. These lights may be arranged in figures of design, such as a circle or rosette or in lines or incorporated in the pattern of an ornamental plaster ceiling. In a church of modern design such lights may be set in a modern abstract pattern.

A church may get along with lantern or general lighting only, but if this is supplemented by specific lighting for each area, when used in the various parts of the service, artificial light may be made a great aid to worship. It is not only desirable to have good reading light and to have a good general light to beautify the architecture, but light can assist in the service if the altar, pulpit, or choir are accentuated as the service places emphasis on these parts of the church.

Different denominations have different lighting needs because of the diversity in their forms of service, and thus the emphasis is on various parts of the church. In the Roman Catholic, Episcopal, and Lutheran churches the emphasis is on the altar, while in many non-liturgical churches the emphasis is on the pulpit; and, in the case of the Christian Science church, the attention is on two pulpits, or desks.

Since lighting the pulpit or reading desk is common to all denominations, we will consider it first. In the past, the pulpit was lighted by one overhead light; then the reading light attached to the desk was produced. This desk light gives light for reading but reflects on the face in an unnatural way, and if the speaker wears glasses his expression is ruined by the reflections on the glasses. A light fastened to a pulpit canopy is so close to the speaker's head that shadows are cast on his face whenever his head moves. The proper light for the pulpit consists of light from two sources so that there are no shadows. This may be an amber light, or one light may be rose and one amber to give a natural appearance to the face. If the minister is bald, the lighting must be regulated so that there are not too many highlights on the bald head. Correct illumination will bring out the changes of expression and gesture and thus make it easier for the congregation to follow the sermon. When a lectern is used, it should also be illuminated by a spotlight as well as by a light on the lectern desk.

Chancel and sanctuary lighting is of utmost importance in the Roman Catholic, Episcopal, and Lutheran churches. The lighting of the sanctuary is a complex problem as it involves the illumination of the altar, the steps, and the communion rail. Many textures, colors, and different materials are used in the sanctuary and each requires a different lighting solution. The light that is necessary for reading may not be the proper light for the mural above the altar. If the altar itself is marble, it will require a different light than an altar covered with a brocaded frontal. Carved or sculptured altars are greatly affected by light and best lighted when the light comes from above and to the side so that no shadows are cast. The intensity and concentration of the light must always be varied with the type of altar. An altar with intricate design should have concentrated light, where an altar of large proportions and bold outline or strong color may be illuminated by a more general light. If marble, mosaic, or metals are used, the light must be arranged to avoid reflections. Indeed, reflection is an important factor in church illumination. Reflected radiation depends on the character of the surface, and the angles of reflection must be carefully controlled when surfaces have a high reflection such as mosaics or metals.

A warm amber light should be used on a white altar or reredos. The light on a carved reredos should be directed so as to bring out the design without awkward shadows or spotting.

Where there are murals, a very pale straw-colored light will best preserve the blues, greens, reds and flesh tones.

Church of St. Clement, Episcopal, Alexandria, Virginia. This church, which has no windows, is illuminated by a pattern of pinpoint lights in the ceiling and spotlights to pick up focal points. To emphasize the mystery of the overbrooding presence of God, the ceiling is painted black and the choir wall dark blue—thus all variations of light and darkness, weather, and sound are shut out. Joseph H. Saunders, architect.

For the use of the priest, the lights on the altar should come from two directions so that his movements cast no shadows. Also there should be sufficient light at the altar rail for the distribution of the communion. The light on the altar steps may be dim, but there must be enough light to avoid accidents. In the Episcopal service, the choir, acolytes, and clergy use the chancel steps both at the processional and recessional. The steps are also used by the congregation at the communion service.

The most effective sanctuary and chancel lighting is by means of reflector lamps concealed behind the chancel arch or from reflectors concealed above the chancel. However, when the structure of the church does not permit concealment, hanging lantern shields may be placed a few feet in front of the lower altar step and at a height to avoid casting shadows on the altar. These lanterns may be fitted with globes on two circuits, to vary the intensity of the light to suit the different parts of the service. The use of reflector lights behind shields will also serve to illuminate a low reredos.

Church services which include a processional and recessional need a different light when this part of the service is taking place. Since the congregation also sings at this time, the light must be for reading. The choir stalls, which are usually in the chancel in the late nineteenth- and early twentieth-century Episcopal churches, require sufficient light for reading at all times, but the light must not be so strong that it detracts from the altar.

Whatever the lighting plan, for the sake of the sexton, it should be as simple as possible. Too many switches and too many circuits would require special training on the part of the person who runs the switchboard. Maintenance is also an important part of lighting, since no matter how much is spent on the lighting system it will not function as it should if there are burned out bulbs. Thus, where possible, fixtures should be installed so that it is not too difficult to replace bulbs.

Colored light may be used in churches, but it must be used with care so that it will not be too dramatic. It is possible to change the color of

First Presbyterian Church, Findlay, Ohio. This traditional Georgian church has light gray-green walls, off-white wainscot, and Fiberglass curtains. The dossal is deep red and gold. The floors are covered with green rubber tile and the aisle carpet is dark gray-green. The brushed brass lighting fixtures, designed by Lewis Smith & Co., are copies of traditional Georgian fixtures. Charles F. Cellarius, architect.

St. George's Church and Friary, Roman Catholic, Seattle, Washington. An example of a combination of indoor and outdoor night lighting. Paul Thiry, architect.

light between the nave and the chancel to help focus the attention, but this must not be so obvious that it is noticeable to the congregation. Blue lights should never be used in a church as they are cold. However, incandescent lamps with blue filters give a daylight quality. Pink light is mellow and creates a restful and comfortable atmosphere. Yellow is the light of sunlight and, for this reason, light from pale straw to amber is the best light. Pale, undiffused light is best for blue or green surfaces. Even a frosted bulb changes colors. The true colors of paintings are brought out by plain, unfiltered light.

Illumination in the church should first of all be efficient and suitable, but there is a wide scope for the illumination consultant with an artistic imagination. Light can be used as design. The most artistic lighting systems in traditional Gothic churches today are those of St. Thomas Church and the Church of the Heavenly Rest, New York City. The methods of lighting in each church vary enough to make a description of each interesting.

The Church of the Heavenly Rest, New York City, built over twenty-five years ago, has a lighting system which was revolutionary at the time it was installed and which is even now a step ahead of the lighting in most churches today. There are no visible lighting fixtures and no floodlights from the ceiling. Instead, a system of floodlights from concealed sources is used. These are arranged under the windows, high on the side walls and back of the parapets of the narrow arcades on both sides of the nave. They project light across the church and upon the opposite walls from which it is reflected as though daylight entered through the windows. Under the windows are 500-watt reflectors of the flood type (six units, three on each side). These project light across the nave and down to five feet from the floor. They cast no shadow. The light decreases as it ascends, and the ceiling is lost in the darkness of infinity. At the side ends of the pews are floods placed in boxes which light the columns. The chancel is lit from reflectors in the arch (two on each side). These are directed on the altar so that no shadow is cast by the priest. The top of the chancel arch has reflectors which light the reredos. A great variety of illumination is possible by the use of the dimming system.

St. Thomas Episcopal Church, New York City, is also of Gothic architecture and is one of the most beautiful churches in America. However, un-

First Evangelical Church, Santa Ana, California. An example of effective night lighting. Frederick Hodgdon, architect.

til recently, much of its beauty was lost under too low or misplaced illumination. Under the direction of Lewis Smith, lighting consultant, the church lighting has been redesigned The old chandeliers, which harmonize with the architecture, have been retained, but they have been redesigned to include the proper sockets which hold projector floodlights on a dimmer system and are directed at the proper angles for reading. There is also an additional socket to provide light for general illumination. The globes are of light amber and give a reading light of 10 watts. The chandeliers are wired on two circuits. The principal source of illumination for the center body of the nave is from a 500-watt spotlight in the triforium gallery hidden behind the vertical columns of each arched opening. The choir area is lighted by down lights in the triforium. The reredos is lighted by ten 500-watt fresnel lens units, five on each side, placed in the organ gallery. These· have amber-color filters graduating in intensity and color from high at the lower part of the reredos to a gradually diminishing level and color at the upper part. The altar is brought out in sharper contrast by two spotlights so focused and shuttered that they frame the altar and dossal behind it. The pulpit and lectern are also spotlighted to illuminate the face of the speaker and the carving on the front part of the pulpit. This lighting is varied throughout the service by a dimmer system similar to that used at the Church of the Heavenly Rest.

Many other churches now use the same remote control dimming system, which is most effective. There is a remote control panel whereby the intensity of the lights can be increased or decreased gradually at any given level. The plan used has low intensity lights before the beginning of the service and during the organ prelude. When the service begins with the Processional, all lights are increased to full intensity or approximately 10 foot-candles. This level of illumination remains until time for the sermon. When the rector enters the pulpit, the nave and choir area lights are dimmed to a low level of intensity and a spotlight is gradually turned on the pulpit to focus the attention on the sermon. If the lectern is used during the service, a spotlight is focused there. After the sermon the pulpit spot is gradually dimmed and the nave lights are gradually increased, but not to full intensity, thus leaving the attention on the choir during the offertory hymn. After the offering, the nave lights are increased to full intensity and remain so to the end of the service. All of this dimming is performed with dignity and solemnity and the transition from high to low intensity is so gradual that the congregation is not conscious of the changes.

Fluorescent lighting is now being used in many churches, but there are many factors that make it unsatisfactory for the church. First of all, fluorescent lights are bad for architecture since they allow for no light and shade. Also fluorescent lamps are cold, because of the blue in them. Some correction has been made for this by the quantalite shield which helps to restore the natural balance of color. Without a shield, the fluorescent lamp causes color distortion. It is possible to dim a fluorescent light, but the effect as the light goes on is mechanical. In addition to the fact that fluorescent lights are expensive maintenance, it is very difficult to design a fixture that is suitable for use in a church, and a special design is necessary so as not to cut the vertical lines prevalent in church architecture.

The church of modern style architecture presents new problems in lighting. Traditional lighting is out of keeping with modern architecture, and stock fixtures which are of period design have no place in the modern church. The best lighting in this style church will be indirect—by means of floods and spots—and should be planned together with the architect so that the illumination can be made a part of the design. Parts of the structure can be made to cast shadows that enhance the architectural plan.

In modern church architecture, natural light from windows is often used dramatically. An early example of this is the light from clerestory windows above the chancel in the Church of the Epiphany, built in New York City in 1936. In one modern church design, a skylight of amber-tinted glass extends above the center of the chancel giving a natural and yet dramatic light. In churches of modern design, the east wall of the sanctuary is often one big window from floor to ceiling of clear or clouded glass, without ornamentation. This brings in the morning light which streams dramatically in a shaft across the altar. Such an arrangement adds spiritually to the service. A church on such an asymmetrical plan should have indirect lighting, and if any fixtures are visible they will be on one side of the nave only, balanced on the other side by light from concealed sources. In some modern churches, even the cross is placed off center, with the altar the only feature on center axis. In such churches it is of course necessary that any visible light fixtures be designed (preferably by the architect) so that they are an integral part of the structure of the building.

In the church of contemporary design, the cross is often illuminated so that it casts a shadow on the wall or it may be illuminated from behind. This is especially effective to relieve or soften the appearance of a simple undecorated wooden, stone, steel, or aluminum cross. This use of light

Plainfield Methodist Church, Plainfield, Iowa. Dramatic lighting on simple stone altar and steel cross. Schweikher and Elting, architects.

is no more theatrical than the use of stained glass windows which give the dim religious light that we have become so accustomed to that we no longer feel the drama and mood of mysticism which they invoke.

Church programs today are expanding to meet the needs of those whose duties make it impossible for them to attend services in the daytime. Thus we have not only the old-fashioned Wednesday night prayer meeting, but also there are often meetings and services in the church or parish house on Tuesday, Thursday, Friday, Saturday, and Sunday. This means there must be adequate lighting for the evening as well as for the daytime. Naturally there must be some exterior, as well as interior, illumination in the evening. The steps and doorway, as well as the bulletin board, must be lighted. There is added welcome when such architectural features as the entrance façade or the church tower or spire are lighted. Also such features as the cross or a stained glass window may be lighted by floods and spotlights. These lights may be placed in the shrubbery or on the building itself. A stained glass window lighted by floods directed on the darkest glass on the inside balcony appears to be evenly lighted on the outside. Stained glass windows in city churches that are near buildings so that no sunlight can reach them can be lighted by floods placed on the exterior rims of the windows so that the colors of the windows will show up in the church interior. These suggestions for exterior illumination are to emphasize parts of the architecture of the church. Such objects as electric crosses are to be frowned upon as they are too closely related to the electric sign.

Architect's drawing of the building plan of the Church of St. John the Divine, Costa Mesa, California. Frederick Hodgdon, architect.

9

Decorative Textiles for the Church

THE decorative importance of textiles in the church cannot be overestimated, because it is largely due to the use of textiles that effect and color are gained. From a practical standpoint, draperies and upholstery materials are needed to furnish churches of all denominations. If there are windows, they may require draperies to modulate the light as well as to enhance the setting, as in churches of Georgian architecture. Arches and doorways often require draperies. Such use of drapery materials will not only add color and pattern, but will also soften the austerity. Draperies may also be used to screen off certain areas when not needed. However, let me add a word about the overuse of draperies, such as curtains looped and hung at the sides of the chancel, which give the effect of a theater curtain. Also heavy folds of drapery material hung at spaced intervals along a brick wall may give a "lived in" feeling to the church, but they certainly do not enhance the architecture or add any spiritual quality.

In choosing draperies or other textiles for the church, you should consider first of all the type of building. Does it follow a definite style of architecture? What are the materials used in the construction of the walls, the floors, the ceiling? Is the general expression one of simplicity and ruggedness or one of ornate refinement? Are the textures smooth or rough? Such considerations will tell us what kind of textiles to look for. If it is a simple country church, for example, we should consider cotton, woolen, and linen materials instead of shiny silks and rayons and metallics. We should look for texture weaves, such as knobby, strip, and basket weaves which have coarseness and weight that harmonize with brick walls and simple wood panelling. Stone walls and marble floors will require the extra richness of velours, velvets, and damasks.

The color scheme of the church has of course been decided upon by the time draperies or upholstery materials are being chosen, and this will limit the choice of the colors for the draperies and pew and chair cushions. Color may be used in draperies and upholstery to accent the other colors by contrast or to form a neutral setting for bright colors in stained glass windows or a mural painting or mosaic.

For example, draperies may be the same color as the walls, but darker in tone, thus giving a pleasing light and dark contrast, but remaining a part of the background. The pew cushions may be tan or gold, and add light to dark wood pews, but by their neutral color they will not interfere with the color scheme. On the other hand,

Wall hanging of appliqué cloth for the feast of Christ the King. (Grailville design)

Green silk crepe chasuble, stole, and maniple, with wool embroidery. (Grailville design)

ancient and Renaissance design are no more appropriate than a baroque altar when used in the church of contemporary modern design.

Scale is also important when choosing textiles for use in the church. Generally speaking, the scale should be in relation to the size of the church and to the size of the piece of furniture to be upholstered. In a large church large, bold pattern is permissible. A large pattern of one color may be used when it blends with the background, while a large bold pattern in a material with contrasting colors would not be the thing to use.

Each building and each room has its own individuality and its own problems of lighting and color. Both drapery and upholstery materials should be selected and tried in the place where they are to be used. Nothing smaller than the standard yard and a half sample will give you any idea of the final effect, and when possible it is better to have a larger sample—a full length of drapery material or enough upholstery material to completely cover the chair or cushion.

Black faille stole, burse, veil, and maniple with linen embroidery. (Grailville design)

the pew cushions may be red or green, and in this case they take a positive place in the color scheme and must be made to match or harmonize with the other colors used in the decorations.

The pattern of the textiles used in the church is also important. Pattern should be appropriate in design. Flashy zig-zags and stripes are not suitable in the church. However, it is not necessary to choose a formal damask or a "church" design since many modern weaves and textures are unobtrusive and thus appropriate, especially in a church of modern design. To have perfect harmony between modern architecture and modern textiles, there must not only be modern weaves, but a new interpretation of design motifs. Indeed there is no reason why religious symbolism such as the symbols of the apostles and saints and even the Trinity and such symbols as IHS cannot be woven in distinctive modern designs so that they harmonize with the expressions of contemporary church architecture. Damasks and brocades of

Price and wearing qualities of materials are also important factors in their choice. Since labor costs on both draperies and upholstery are so high, the best quality material is cheaper in the long run, since it will not have to be replaced so often. Draperies must be of a quality that will not fade. If there are metal threads, they should be tarnish proof. The material should not shrink with cleaning nor should it lose its body. Upholstery materials for the church should stand hard wear. They should be of a weave or pattern that will not show dirt or spots too easily. Another precaution is to buy extra yardage for replacement, or for such an enlargement project as extra pews, which will need matching seat cushions.

Materials appropriate for church draperies include silk, cotton, or wool damasks. These are usually made in dignified, formal designs and come in a variety of colors which will harmonize with most any color scheme. They hang in graceful folds. Imported Italian damasks in conventional designs stamped on cotton have a hand blocked effect and thus have exceptional decorative value. They are made in widths of 50 inches and narrower and some have combinations of gold and silver with color. Damasks are made in both large and small all-over patterns and a quality suitable for church purposes costs from $5 a yard up, for a material 50 inches in width. All draperies of this type should be lined to protect them and made double fullness to hang properly.

Cotton, nylon, and silk velvets are also good for church draperies. Velvets range in price from $3.50 a yard for a cotton velvet, $6.50 for nylon velvet, $8.25 for water repellent cotton velvet, up to $25 a yard for a silk velvet. Velvet draperies should be lined and should have double yardage for fullness. There are also linens and cottons with heavy textures and synthetic materials with new weaving effects which are suitable for draperies. However, a loose-woven material may sag when hung in heavy lengths of drapery. For this reason such material as monk's cloth is not always satisfactory, while a closer weave such as poplin or denim will not sag. There are also new synthetic materials that filter the sunshine, yet offer texture interest. These materials could be used in some of the new churches that have large expanse of windows.

Upholstery materials are required for pew cushions, benches, and chairs, and for kneelers when such are used in the service.

Upholstery materials suitable for church wear

A chasuble by Henri Matisse. Red satin with yellow silk and black velvet ribbon appliqué. From the Museum of Modern Art, Design Collection, New York City. Gift of Mrs. Charles Suydam Cutting.

Angels—needlework, fifty by sixty inches, by Mariska Karasz.

include wool damasks, cotton and wool tapestries, wool poplins, and mohair and frieze. All of these materials have excellent wearing qualities and are made in both plain and patterned designs which include small diamond all-over patterns, large and small damask patterns, and textured effects. The best wearing upholstery material is frieze. There are mohair friezes and nylon and cotton friezes and mothproof friezes. Mohairs and friezes range from $12 to $20 a yard for 50-inch material. A mohair has a cut surface while the frieze loops are uncut so will never mat down. Cotton tapestries, which wear excellently, come in plain colors and range from $10 a yard up in price. Imported tapestries with small patterns or centered designs range from $12 a yard to $24 a yard. There are also cotton moquettes which give good wear. The most important factor about an upholstery material is that it have a strong, close weave and a comparatively hard, even surface. Uneven weaves and textures are not good for church upholstery.

Upholstery for church pews and kneeling cushions should have a good firm pad. If foam rubber is used, it should be of the best quality and of a thickness that will not sink under the heaviest weight. Foam rubber cushions are baked into shape, but this is not always permanent. The best padding for upholstery and church kneelers is kopac, since it will hold its firmness for many years and is also comfortable. Leather kneelers with pressed cork padding are hard and uncomfortable to the knees.

In the liturgical church, textiles play an important part in the setting of the service. The liturgical textiles used in Episcopal and Lutheran churches include dossal and riddel curtains, frontals and frontlets, the burse and veil for the chalice, and vestments for the ministers. The Roman Catholic Church uses textiles for vestments, for the baldachin, and for tabernacle curtains, as well as frontals and other curtains about the altar.

The dossal curtain, when used, hangs on the wall behind the altar. The riddels or side curtains are fastened to posts around the altar. Damasks and brocades are also used for vestments and for the chalice burse and veil. The pulpit and lectern falls and book marks and banners are all made of

Tapestry for Temple Aushe Chesed, Cleveland, Ohio, by Abraham Rattner. Design of cream with gold thread, yellow, green, orange, reds, blacks, browns, and pinks on dark blue ground.

Dalmatic of red corded silk, lined in blue with velvet appliqué bands of black, green, and white velvet. Designed for Trinity Church, New York City, by the Rev. Canon Edward N. West. Made by J. M. Hall.

various textiles, as is the funeral pall.

The colors of liturgical textiles follow the color sequence in use in your individual church. All liturgical textiles in use on any particular day should match as nearly as possible. They must be the same color such as green, red, white, or purple, and are certainly more harmonious if they are the same shade of the color. For example, if the dossal is a Kelly green and the minister's chasuble is an olive green, it is not as pleasing as when the greens match. However, the use of gold and silver and brocade bandings and borders helps to blend the colors.

Liturgical textiles are usually of silk damask, but they may also be of other materials such as silk rep. They may also be of brocade or of hand embroidery or may have hand painted or needlework orphreys.

The form as well as the color of liturgical textiles is prescribed by the rubrics of the church and follows traditional usage. However, the decora-

tion and the materials may vary according to taste and to appropriateness with the furnishings of your particular church.

Traditionally, silk damasks and brocades are the materials used for these articles. From the earliest times, the history of decorative silks has been tied in with the church. Not only were the materials woven for church use, but the motifs of design and the subject matter were taken from church symbolism and biblical sources. Some of the earliest silk fabric designs include Joseph and his Brethren, Daniel in the Lions' Den, the Annunciation, and the Birth of Christ.

Byzantine fabrics of the sixth and seventh centuries show lions and other animals, and by the thirteenth century we find Italian silks used for baldachin fabrics with designs of eagles, lions, griffins, and other animals in circles. Also such secular scenes as horsemen hunting and leopards, elephants, and hounds were used. Romanesque silk brocades of the thirteenth century include designs of the Birth of Christ, the Virgin Mary and Angels, St. Nicholas and the Virgin, and the Crucifixion. These biblical subjects continued to be woven in the silks made in Italy, France, and Cologne—silk weaving centers down through the Middle Ages.

Gothic silks were woven in such designs as the large pomegranate and artichoke, the eagle, griffin, hounds, lions, and later the vase pattern. Most any of these designs, up until the eighteenth century, when they become too secular in inspiration, are suitable for church usage. Many of the old designs have been reproduced, such as the

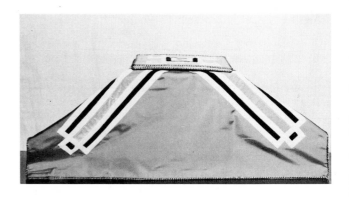

Burse and veil to match dalmatic shown above.

Venetian fifteenth-century design of stags under radiant clouds.

Other designs with religious symbols have been adapted especially for the church. These are made in rayon damask and in the church colors—white, black, red, olive green, and violet. The designs include the Agnus Dei (with the IHS and Lamb); the Tudor Rose; the Hosanna (with angels and Chi Rho); a design of roses, crown, and rays; and another design of the passion flower, known under the trade name of Normandy. Then there are several all-over repeat patterns which include the Cross in various forms, or the Trinity symbol of interlaced circles; the hart or 42nd Psalm, the four evangelists, and the threefold office of Christ, a design with grapes, crowns, and the Chi Rho. Many of these patterns are available with metallic gold or silver, and some, such as the stags under radiant clouds, must be made to order in silk, although a rayon copy is available.

Red silk crepe chasuble with silk embroidery. (Grailville design)

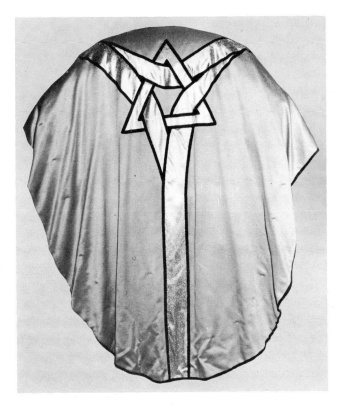

Chasuble of green antique satin, with design of gold and silver metal cloth outlined in black and lined in gold silk. Designed for Trinity Church, New York City, by the Rev. Canon Edward N. West.

Some of these special ecclesiastical designs are in good taste, but some are garish and many designs chosen from regular stock are often more effective. There are imported silk damasks without sheen, and there are soft wool and linen damasks, and imported printed cotton damasks which are artistic and beautiful for church use. Also many plain satins and corded silks are suitable and effective for church hangings and vestments. The use of liturgical fabrics will be treated in more detail in the chapter on "Altar and Sanctuary Furnishings."

Drapery and upholstery materials, for use in church offices, the ladies' parlor, and various rooms in the parish house can be left to individual taste—except that we must remember that each room has its own individuality and purpose. The lighting and exposure of each room is different and this will determine the colors to be used. The room with north light can be made to seem

Liturgical drape in appliqué and embroidery, 18 feet high, designed for a baptistry. (Grailville design)

is too high. Large bold patterns are for rooms of large proportions. All these questions of color and scale are important when choosing material for draperies or upholstery materials.

It is also well to be conservative in the choice of pattern for draperies so that the people who see them every day will not get tired of them. It is the same principle as the flashy dress and the basic model. Only those who have many clothes and do not have to wear them more than one season can afford the flashy model. Nor do we mean that draperies and upholstery in the church buildings must be drab and uninteresting. Rather they should have the wearing quality of conservative good taste. But they may also be cheerful and gay.

Draperies and upholstery materials must be related in color to the walls, to the rug, and to each other to tie the whole room together. Draperies can be the same color as the walls. This will make a room look larger. Draperies too light in color should be avoided in public rooms which get a great deal of wear and use.

Whether the draperies should be figured or plain depends upon the rest of the room. If the

Black faille chasuble with linen embroidery. (Grailville design)

warmer and more cheerful if warm colors such as yellows, oranges, and reds are used with small amounts of cool blues and greens. A small room can be made to seem larger by the use of cool colors which make the walls seem farther away. Also plain materials or materials with small patterns are best in a small room. In a room with low ceiling, drapery material with vertical stripes, or with a pattern which has an upward movement, will give the room apparent height. Horizontal lines will seem to cut the height of a ceiling that

86

rug is figured, the draperies should be plain; if the floor is plain, figured draperies may be used. In choosing upholstery fabrics, plain materials, stripes, and patterned materials may be used on different pieces of furniture in the same room, but in quantity of surface covered one pattern and one color must dominate. Thus you could use an all-over repeat pattern of one color on the large sofa and different colors and patterns on each of several chairs. An example of the use of color and pattern for a ladies' parlor might include plain tan walls and woodwork, brown asphalt tile floor, chintz draperies with tans, brown, green, and orange. Sofa in plain green; a chair in green, tan, and orange stripe; and side chairs in orange material with a small diamond repeat pattern.

If the furniture and background of a room are a certain style, the fabrics should harmonize in style as well as color. Thus if the room's furnishings are Colonial, the drapery and upholstery materials might include calico-patterned chintz and textured homespuns. A room with English period furniture might use hand-blocked linen draperies, tapestry weave upholstery, and also stripe designs, while nubby textures, horizontal stripes, and plain materials are harmonious with modern furniture. Any of these styles may be used in decorating the various rooms of the parish house. The best quality materials should be chosen, since labor costs of both draperies and upholstery are so expensive that the draperies or upholstery

should not have to be replaced too often. Figured linens are excellent for draperies, because their texture wears and seems to shed dust and dirt. Also a good linen chintz when it fades will still look well for many years.

Furniture upholstered in materials with a small all-over repeat pattern will stand more wear than plain material. A hard-surface, close-woven material will also wear better than one that is too nobby and loosely woven.

Draperies should be hung floor length, with ample fullness, and should be lined. The lining may be cream-color sateen or it may be one of the dark colors in the material, which will show less dirt. The top finish may be a plain valance of material for a wooden cornice or a wooden or metal pole. Glass curtains are not necessary, but some draperies in certain rooms may want to be made to pull across the window if there are no venetian or other blinds at the windows.

The information given in this chapter does not mean that the guild should take over the making of draperies or the upholstery of pews or other furniture. It can be done when necessary. However, the more informed the layman is in such matters the better service he can get from the professional decorator. Also, although large cities have decorators who specialize in church decoration, there are many small churches that are far from large cities or cannot afford to have the work done by a hired decorator.

Architect's drawing of St. Elizabeth's Episcopal Church, Seahurst, Washington. Durham, Anderson, and Freed, architects.

The sanctuary of St. Brigid's Roman Catholic Church, Los Angeles, California. The wall is mosaic, the floor terrazzo. The tabernacle, candlesticks, and altar ornament by Hudson Roysher.

10

Altar and Sanctuary Furnishings

IN THE liturgical churches, such as the Roman Catholic, Episcopal, and Lutheran, there are a great many more furnishings which demand decorative treatment than in the non-liturgical church. These include the liturgical fittings for the altar and sanctuary. These appointments are governed by their use in the service. They should also harmonize with the architecture of the building and the other furnishings of the church—although the form and function of liturgical appointments is determined by the church. Their design and fabrication also require expert knowledge. Such articles as crosses, croziers, chalices, patens, ciboria, tabernacles, candlesticks and candelabra, hanging altar lamps, and censers all require the work of experts. Vestments and altar hangings also require experts with special knowledge of church rules as well as the know-how in their own particular field.

The altar cross and candlesticks remain on the altar whether there is a service or not so they must be counted as part of the church decoration. The cross and candlesticks should match each other in material and design and all should be in harmony with the general scheme of the church architecture and decoration. The altar cross and candlesticks may be made of any material from simple iron, brass, copper, stone, terra cotta, or wood, to silver, gold, crystal, or enamel inlaid with precious stones. The material will be determined by the architecture of the church. In a large church of impressive architecture, a silver cross and candlesticks are suitable. A small fieldstone church could have a wrought iron cross and candlesticks, while a simple brick or wooden church could have cross and candlesticks of terra cotta. An adobe or plaster church in Arizona or New Mexico could have a wooden cross and candle-

sticks with bold color decoration, or cross and candlesticks of Indian hammered silver design studded with native turquoise. For a church in the desert, what could be more suitable than a cross and candlesticks carved from bleached desert wood and stained in the manner of the primitive wood sculptures from the islands of the Pacific? These suggestions are made in an effort to stimulate the imaginative to thinking in terms outside the wholesale catalog products of brass.

There are beautiful crosses and candlesticks made of enamel. Many of these, as well as crosses and candlesticks of rock crystal with gold bands, are to be seen in museum collections. This combination of crystal and gold might well be used again today. Silver and ebony are combined, and ivory and ebony, or ivory and silver, make beautiful combinations for altar crosses and candle-

Altar cross and candlesticks of brass and African vermilion wood, designed and executed by Hudson Roysher for Claremont Congregational Church, Claremont, California.

89

The cross above the altar of St. Mark's Episcopal Church, St. Louis, Missouri. Made of pewter, brass, and red leather. Designed by Frederick Dunn, architect.

sticks. The altar cross should be large in proportion to the candlesticks, and the candlesticks, while matching the cross in design, should never be as ornate.

The altar cross was originally designed for the use of the clergy and ought always to rest upon the altar itself. The great crucifix on the rood screen was the focus of the people's attention, but since most rood screens have been done away with, the cross on the altar has to serve both clergy and people. This has led to the use of the stepped cross or the cross on a tabernacle-like structure which tends to dwarf the other appointments.

A large cross on the wall above the altar also serves as an altar cross. The cross on the wall may be of wood, stone, or any metal or it may be painted on the wall or inlaid in the wall, such as the beautiful marble mosaic cross in St. Bartholomew's Church, New York City. If the cross is suspended, it should be in relation to the altar and not be hung too high above it or forward in space and thus not a part of the altar grouping. The cross on the sanctuary wall should be large and should be the dominant feature on the wall. It should not get lost among the carved figures of saints or the mural decoration. Especially fine examples of stone crosses set in the wall or reredos behind the altar are to be seen in the Church of the Heavenly Rest and St. Thomas Church, New York City. The suspended cross should also be large, but not so large that it seems to be heavier than the altar. It may be of carved, or polychromed wood or of metal.

The processional cross may be simple or ornate in design and may be of any material that harmonizes with the spirit of the other church decorations. Processional candlesticks are usually of wood with metal cups and are quite simple in design. The pavement lights which are set in the sanctuary on either side and to the front may be of iron or bronze, or even of wood. They must be heavy and firm so that they will not fall over. They usually hold several candles in the manner of a candelabra.

The Paschal candle, which is used only at the Easter season, must have its own candlestick and while it should be heavy enough to insure safety, it must be removable. For this reason, it is best that the Paschal candlestick be of wood rather than metal. The Paschal candlestick is placed on the north side of the sanctuary and is lighted from Easter Even until Ascension Day. Paschal candlesticks were often so tall that the candle had to be lit through a hole in the roof. Their design included figures of the Virgin and a cross. The candle itself is wax and is marked with a cross and five grains of incense.

Sanctuary lamps should conform strictly to the architectural style of the church. For this reason, the modern church building will perhaps require an original design since most stock sanctuary lamps are usually too ornate. Pewter, aluminum, or brass are the most satisfactory metals for sanctuary lamps.

Church appointments such as crosses and candlesticks, tabernacles, reliquaries, and croziers are among the treasured articles in museums all over the world. Although there are many equally fine works of art done for churches today, the tendency is toward simplicity of design. This does not mean that the workmanship should be shoddy or that the factory can do a plain piece just as well. On the contrary, it demands more careful designing, with the emphasis—as in contemporary architecture—on proportion and form rather than ornate detail.

The crozier, which is the pastoral staff carried by a bishop, has been made in several distinct traditional forms which are followed today. Early croziers consisted of a short staff with a ball or knob. Croziers were also made with crutch or Tau cross head. Later the staff had a head with a simple curve like a walking stick and this in turn developed into a crook turned on an inward spiral, often ending with an animal head. Croziers have been made of materials such as iron, pewter, copper, wood, horn, and bronze, but precious materials such as silver and gold, with decorations of ivory, rock crystal, enamel, and precious stones, were more often used.

Tabernacles and reliquaries have always been articles of beautiful workmanship—whether of colorful enamel or plain silver or other metal.

Vases for altar flowers should be of the same material as the altar cross and candlesticks or they may be of clear glass. The average altar vase today is a poor container for flowers and is also not too pleasing in design. Vases should have a wide mouth so that flowers can be arranged properly. Also there should be space to put a flower holder in the bottom of the vase and enough depth for water and for long-stemmed flowers.

The chalice, paten, ciborium, wafer box, cruets, flagon, and lavabo used for the communion service are usually of silver, although in the past they have been made of such materials as wood, pewter, bronze, crystal, agate, or even gold. The chalice and the paten should match for they must be designed to use together. It is also well to have a ciborium which will hold enough wafers for such services as Christmas and Easter. The ciborium should also be designed to match the chalice.

The use of these communion appointments dictates their form. The bowl of the chalice should be shallow enough to permit the communicant to drink from it easily; the knob should be of a size that can be held firmly by the celebrant and its surface should be smooth so that it will not catch on things. The base should be large enough and heavy enough to prevent its being upset. Within these limits, the decoration and materials may vary. The chalice, being the most important vessel, should set the pattern for the other articles. A silver chalice may have a knob of ivory, gold, crystal, or semi-precious or precious stones or the base may have ornamentation of enamel or precious stone insets. There may be variations in the depth and shape of the bowl and in the length and design of the stem and also in the form and decoration of the base. The design of the chalice form changes with the variation in the size and depth of the bowl and the length of the stem and size of the base, as well as the location and size of the knob. The average chalice is from 7 to 10 inches tall. If the chalice is made taller, it may seem top-heavy. There are no rules governing the

An altar cross of wood and gesso, with polychrome of gold, silver, and blue, designed for St. John's Episcopal Church, Tuckahoe, New York, by the Rev. Canon Edward N. West.

decoration of the chalice. It may be covered with detailed silverwork or a combination of gold and silver, or it may be set with jewels or colored enamel. If jewels are used, a great variety of colors are possible in both precious and semi-precious stones. Imitations should never be used. For purple, there is the amethyst; the tourmaline and peridot give green; and the onyx and malachite, opaque green. The garnet and ruby can be used for red; the sapphire, the zircon, and the lapis-lazuli for turquoise and aquamarine blue. The carnelian gives brown and reds; the topaz and amber, yellow; the onyx, black; and rock crystal and the diamond can be used for white. Stones should never be set in sharp claw settings. However, the decoration should be concentrated in one place such as the knob or base or in a medallion on the bowl. The same rules of design should be served in the other matching appointments, but they should be much less ornate than the chalice.

All these altar fittings require the work of specialists and craftsmen. However, as beautiful as each article may be itself, someone must oversee the completion of all of these furnishings and tie them in with the appearance of the church as a whole. The architect is the one who knows what type of cross belongs on the altar which he designed and actually he is the one who should design it. At least he should be able to make a rough sketch which could be turned over to the artist or craftsman who will do the work. It is the architect who is trained to avoid the use of Gothic lighting fixtures in a modern church and he should see that all the details in the church are right. Indeed, it is as much the architect's job to see that the cross on the altar is of the proper design as it is to select the color of the paint on the walls.

However, the most of these altar appointments are usually given as memorials, since they, of all church fittings, are the most suitable for memorials. But this means that they are often given years after the church is built, so unless they are planned far ahead of time the architect may not

The altar of St. George's Church and Friary, Roman Catholic, Seattle, Washington. Paul Thiry, architect and designer.

even be about for consultation. It is best to include notes on the style and design of possible memorials when the initial church plans are made —thus if someone desires to give a cross the minister could refer to the records. Then he could say, "Yes, we would like to have you give a cross as a memorial. In fact, here is a sketch of one we have been hoping to have for many years." Such procedure would avoid the placing of memorials which may be beautiful in themselves, but are not designed to suit the position in which they are placed.

A wood and gesso processional cross, with polychrome of silver and gold, designed for the United States Military Academy Chapel, West Point, New York, by the Rev. Canon Edward N. West.

The vestments of the church, which include all the articles of liturgical clothing worn by the clergy, as well as the frontals, dossals, riddels, burse, and veil, complete the liturgical furnishing of the altar and sanctuary.

When the full complement of eucharistic vestments are used they should match in color. The burse, veil, and stole should not only match in color, but also should be made of the same material and have the same decoration. However, there is no rule that calls for crosses or other embroidered designs or symbols on either the burse or veil. The veil is usually 24 inches square. It is made of silk damask and lined in contrasting silk. It is usually decorated with a cross at the center front, or may have an orphrey of some church symbol, or it may be embroidered all over. The burse, which holds the linen used in the service, is 9 inches square. It is of damask or corded silk with a design on its top matching that on the veil and should be lined with linen.

The minister's stole which he uses at the communion service should be made of the same damask or corded silk, and decorated with the same symbols, as the burse and veil. There are many symbols that can be used to decorate these liturgical pieces.

Stoles for special occasions such as baptisms, weddings, and other festival days may have more elaborate embroidery, such as roses, angels, alleluia, or grapes for a more decorative eucharistic stole.

Anyone undertaking the making of any liturgical textiles should have a book on church symbols, and the services of an artist who can adapt the designs to the article to be made. Antique damasks and brocades may be used in making such articles as the burse, veil, and stole.

In the past, the chasuble was usually made of damask with a figured pattern and also with orphreys or elaborate design. However, from the decorative standpoint, the general effect in the church is enhanced by a contrast, so that if the other vestments at the altar are of figured textiles, the chasuble could be of a material without pattern and with only color contrast, similar to the modern chasubles made by Matisse. Pugin considers velvet the best material for chasubles, or small-figured silks, since large figures are broken by the orphreys. In a large church such designs would be especially effective.

If the rules of heraldic coloring are followed, the colors will be separated by gold and silver; and gold and silver when used should be separated by color. This rule if followed will keep any vestment, frontal, or dossal, from seeming "loud" even when complementary color contrasts such as red on green are used. In these days of expensive handwork, we should rely on the richness of the fabric itself and the beauty of contrasting linings rather than ornate orphreys of hand embroidery.

Although liturgical vestments can be made by

LEFT: Processional cross in sterling silver and Brazilian rosewood, designed and executed by Hudson Roysher for St. Mary of the Angels Episcopal Church, Hollywood, California.

RIGHT: Silver Chapter Processional Cross designed for the Cathedral Church of St. John the Divine, New York City, by the Rev. Canon Edward N. West.

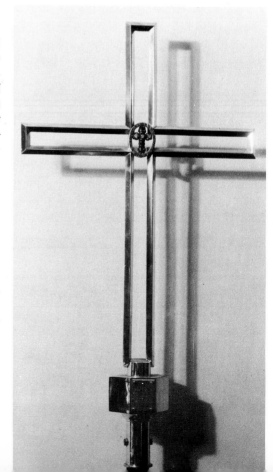

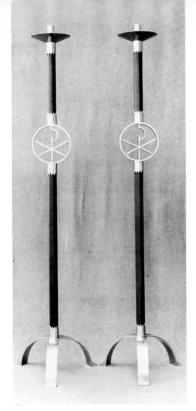

Sanctuary candlesticks of brass and red leather, designed and executed by Hudson Roysher for St. Mark's Episcopal Church, Upland, California.

to a cloth which covers the altar in the same manner as pleated skirts are hung below a bed. The altar frontals should be designed in relation to the dossals which will be in use at the same time. A superfrontal may hang over the frontal. It is usually about nine inches in depth and may be edged in a short fringe and decorated with a border or medallion of embroidery or with contrasting bands of velvet.

There are professional makers of church vestments, altar hangings, and other church vestments in all large cities, but it is possible for a small church to make its own liturgical textiles. However, careful measuring and workmanship is necessary to avoid an amateur job. The dossal, since it is a plain curtain hung on a wall, seems simple to make. However, it should never be attempted unless a large table the size of the dossal itself is available to work on. The material of the dossal must be heavy and it must also have a heavy sateen lining. In order to hang well it must have at least one and one-half widths of fullness, but it may be stretched flat with no fullness. It should have an interlaced cord at the top to hang it onto a rod fastened on the chancel wall. The dossal is more effective if designed with vertical

machine and the effect from a distance will be just the same, handwork, especially in the finishing of the chasuble, is desirable even if the design is as simple as a velvet cross appliquéd on plain ribbed silk. If the appliqué is stitched on, it may pull and thread with use. If such decorations as orphreys are appliquéd, their intricate outline will require hand stitching.

From the liturgical standpoint, no altar can be fully effective without frontals. To be effective, these must be designed with regard to the whole church. Traditionally, there were three types of materials used as altar frontals: metal, wood, and cloth. Metal frontals were of gold and silver, with jewels. Wood frontals were painted and gilt, and in Spain frontals of embossed and gilded leather were used. Cloth frontals may be of gold, velvet, silk embroidered, or damasks. Frontals were also made of woven tapestry and needlepoint. The frontal of cloth, of course, changes color with the season and with the other church vestments. The altar may or may not have a superfrontal.

The altar frontal may be similar to the dossal in design. The frontal covers the altar and hangs to the floor. It is usually flat, without fullness, and may be stretched and fastened on a board which is then fastened to the altar, or it may be fastened

Processional cross to mark the twenty-fifth anniversary of the Rev. Roelif H. Brooks, D.D., as rector of St. Thomas Episcopal Church, New York City. Made of gifts of gold, silver, and precious and semiprecious stones. Designed and executed by Louis F. Glasier.

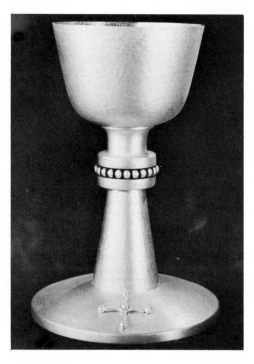

LEFT: Sterling silver chalice with knob enriched with band of beading and small matching cross in base. Designed and executed by Louis F. Glasier.

RIGHT: Sterling silver chalice designed by the Rev. Canon Edward N. West. Executed by Louis F. Glasier.

bands of contrasting color or material such as brocade or velvet on a damask background, or damask on a velvet dossal. Lace and embroidery bands are also permissable. One new church has a screen of dark wood fretwork design back of the altar. The dossal curtain hangs behind this screen and its color changes with the season. The riddels are curtains hung on a rod that ends in decorated posts holding candles at the front ends of the altar. They should be from six to eight feet high. Riddels should match the dossal and the color of riddels changes with the church seasons.

The funeral pall used to cover the coffin at a church funeral should be about 9 x 6 feet. It is made with a lining and is usually of purple, but may be red, white, or black. It is usually of velvet or damask and has a cross which extends the length and width. It may be lined in a contrasting color and edged with gold braid and may have tassels at the corners.

A pulpit or lectern hanging is usually a flat piece of lined damask, square or rectangular to fit the dimensions of the desk. It may have an embroidered symbol such as IHS. The colors follow those prescribed for the day so that you will need hangings in red, green, white, purple, and black, which should match the other liturgical textiles.

Bookmarks should match the pulpit hangings. While all of these vestments and hangings may be made by amateurs (in fact there are kits available) it is best, when possible, to have them made by professionals since the "fit" and "hang" are important. Indeed there is nothing that can upset the beauty and formality of a service more than sloppy and ill-fitting vestments, hangings that do not hang as they should, candles that sputter, or flowers that are the wrong color or poorly arranged in the altar vases. Each detail of the altar appointments should be correct in color, form, and line, and should always be treated with dignity.

Church vestments have usually relied on handwork for their decoration. White linen vestments were embroidered with crosses and other simple symbols and designs. The silk vestments, however, had more elaborate colored embroideries in the form of orphreys. The designs included not only symbols but also figures with biblical scenes. Embroidery not only decorated the priest's vestments, the chasuble, the cope, the stole, and the tippet, but also the vestments of the altar, the frontals, superfrontals, the dossal, and riddel curtains; the chalice vestments of the burse and veil, and the pall that covers the coffin at a funeral.

Many of these articles were made at convents or by groups of church needlewomen in guilds and many were made by devout noblewomen and even queens. However, for some years this work has been done by professionals.

The most of the embroidery used on church vestments is still done by professional needlewomen. There is much beautiful work being done by the small companies and guilds which make church vestments. In Los Angeles, California, the Diocesan Woman's Auxiliary conducts classes of instruction in church embroidery and there are several other such schools. However, the cost and the time element have reduced the amount of embroidery used so that now the design usually consists of a simple cross or symbol with a minimum of surrounding decoration. More elaborately embroidered vestments are still being made in Europe and are imported. Much of the work on white linen vestments and altar linens is done in Puerto Rico.

Other necessary furnishings of the altar and sanctuary include kneelers, cushions, and footpace or sanctuary rugs. Every communion rail needs cushions and the altar steps need kneelers for priests and acolytes. The sedilia, chairs, and prie-dieu in the sanctuary also need cushions and upholstery. A footpace rug before the altar, or a larger sanctuary rug, is also desirable. All of these fittings can be made of commercial fabrics. However, there has been a renaissance in the last ten years to again enrich these altar appointments with handwork.

During the past ten years there has also been a revival of needlepoint for use in the Episcopal churches of America. The first such work that I know of were the kneelers made by Mrs. Stephen F. Bayne for St. Mark's Cathedral, Seattle, Washington. Mrs. Bayne was later instrumental in starting the needlework project for Trinity Church, New York City. Sixty women of Trinity Parish have been working for almost four years making kneelers, communion rail cushions, chair cushions, prie-dieu cushions, and rugs and hangings for the sanctuary of the high altar and of All Saints' Chapel. The backgrounds of all of the pieces are red. Various colors are used in the beautiful symbols and floral designs. In both the

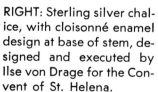

LEFT: Sterling silver chalice designed and executed by Hudson Roysher for St. Paul's Episcopal Church, San Diego, California.

RIGHT: Sterling silver chalice, with cloisonné enamel design at base of stem, designed and executed by Ilse von Drage for the Convent of St. Helena.

Communion rail cushion of All Saints' Chapel of Trinity Church, New York City. The designs are worked in white, gold, and blue on a red background.

designs and the coloring, the colors and details of the altar and reredos decorations have been studied and used, together with the traditional colors of the various symbols.

The cushions for the sedilia at the high altar are designs using flowers of the Bible. There are eight cushions, each with a separate flower design: the carnation, the columbine, the iris or fleur-de-lis, the passion flower, the rose, the violet, the lily of the valley, and the snowdrop. These are especially beautiful in both color and design.

The footpace rug at the high altar has a center medallion of the pelican taken from a mosaic medallion in the altar. The background of the rug is scattered with small roses, and the border is a design of red, green, and purple grapes, adapted from the grape border in the stone reredos.

There are five long altar rail cushions. The center cushion has medallions of the dove, St. Matthew represented by the figure of a man, St. Mark, by the winged lion, St. Luke, by the winged ox, and St. John, by the eagle. The cushions to the left and right of the center cushion have medallions with the symbols of the twelve apostles, while the cushions to the far right and left repeat the designs of the fifteen acolyte kneelers in the sanctuary. All cushions have the grape and grapevine background designs taken from the border in the stone reredos.

The deacon's and sub-deacon's cushion designs are of the Trinity symbol and the symbol of St. Augustine, the name of one of the Chapels of Trinity Parish. The design on the rector's prie-

dieu incorporates the seal of Trinity Parish and the symbols of St. Paul and St. Luke, on a background of grapes and grapevines.

The needlepoint in All Saints' Chapel has a red background with stalks of the white lily and blue fleur-de-lis—the flowers of the Virgin and of royalty. The four kneelers on the altar steps have center shields containing a cross with gold fleur-de-lis and the monogram of the Virgin. The sedilia cushion design has a center motif of a gold crown, the Virgin's monogram, and lilies and gold fleur-de-lis on the red background. The background design of the altar rail cushions also includes lily stalks and fleur-de-lis, and the center medallions are the dove, the lamb, the Virgin's monogram and crown, and the symbol of St. Joseph. The footpace rug also has a red background with white lily stalks and a center gold crown motif. In this chapel are the Bishop's throne and prie-dieu. The designs of these cushions include the seal of the Diocese of New York and passion flowers and vines. This design was also taken from the stone carving of the reredos at the high altar. In addition to these altar pieces, there are tippets for each member of the clergy staff, with the seal of Trinity Parish worked in silk petit point. The designs and cartoons for these pieces were adapted for needlework by Rosetta Larsen.

As long as ten years ago, kneelers of needlepoint were made by the alumni of Rosemary Hall, Greenwich, Connecticut, for the school chapel, St. Bede's, one of the most beautiful small chapels in America. There are also beautiful needlepoint kneelers in the chapel of St. Andrew's School, Wilmington, Delaware.

There are now many excellent needlepoint designers in all sections of America and many skilled needlewomen. In fact the needlepoint revival which began with a few New York woman has now spread to include skilled workers and amateurs in all parts of America.

One of the first churches after Trinity to be furnished with needlework was St. James' Episcopal Church, New York City. The needlepoint kneelers, communion rail cushions, and footpace rug at the high altar were all designed by Mrs. William W. Hoppin, together with Geneva B. Hutchins, a professional needlework designer, and worked by Mrs. Hoppin. The communion rail cushions have a background design of the Christmas rose and the Easter lily adapted from carvings on an old pulpit. The center medallions of the cushions are the chalice, the lamb, the cross, the Holy Spirit, and wheat. The designs of the twelve kneelers are the symbols of the apostles, each set on a cross as a background. The footpace rug incorporates the coat of arms of the church in a quatrefoil shield. An all-over cross pattern forms the background and the inscription "Glory to Thee O Lord" is also worked into the rug. The border of the rug repeats a design in the stone carvings, and the colors were chosen for careful harmony with the colorful reredos.

The communion rail cushions, the kneelers, and rug for the chapel at St. James' Church were made by a group of women of the Parish including Mrs. Eugene W. Stetson. The designs and colors were adapted from *The Sign Language of Our Faith* by Helen Stuart Griffith. The background color is blue to match the mural in the reredos. The colors used all blend with the polychrome reredos and the mural above it. The five communion rail cushions have designs with these symbols: the dove, the Lamb of God, the Hand of God, the pelican, and the twelve apostles' shields. The two side cushions include the rose, the lily, the seven doves, the nine-pointed star, and an arrangement of Greek letters symbolizing Jesus Christ the Victor. The triangular border symbolizes the Trinity. The footpace rug includes a medallion of the shield of the Trinity.

Nearly four hundred women in all parts of the United States, as well as in England and France, are making needlepoint kneelers, cushions, and rugs for the high altar and the nine chapel altars of the National Cathedral in Washington, D. C. The articles for the high altar include seats, backs, and kneelers for the sedilia and for the special stalls as well as the bishop's cathedra. There are also ten altar cushions and a large altar rug and 102 cushions for the choir stalls, each with the seal of a different diocese in the center. All the needlepoint used is symbolic in design and color and when finished the gorgeous ecclesiastical colors will make a spectacular sight. The rug at the high altar is 21 feet long by 80 inches wide,

The Bishop's chair in Trinity Church, New York City. The needlepoint design in the cushion is the seal of the Diocese of New York, surrounded by passion flowers and vines in natural colors on a red background.

The footpace rug of needlepoint worked for the high altar at St. James' Church, New York City, by Mrs. William W. Hoppin, has the shield of St. James on a background of crosses.

and on each side are small rugs 45 by 65 inches, called the Epistle and Gospel rugs. The large rug has a deep cream background with borders of dark green to match the green marble floor. There is a great deal of blue and red and it will give the effect of sun coming through a stained glass window. The design is similar to that of an old Oriental rug except that in the corners there are Jerusalem crosses of the same design as the bronze cross set in the Jerusalem stone altar.

The cushions at the high altar have center symbols of the dove, the lamb, the book, and the flame, on blue backgrounds, with border designs of the lily, rose, grape, and oak.

The sedilia backs have a design of a large cross with the symbols of the four evangelists terminating the ends of the cross. The seat design is a cross against a background of palm leaves, and the kneelers have the IHS symbol and a floral border. The backgrounds are blue and red. There are also special stalls, such as the bishop's, chaplain's, and dean's, and these all have seats and kneelers. The imposing bishop's cathedra made from the stones of Glastonbury Abbey has a seat and back of a design comprising the coat of arms of the Cathedral with a border repeating the stone cutting. The background color of these cushions is stone gray with the designs worked in red and gold. The kneelers, stall cushions, and communion rail cushions of St. Mary's Chapel have a color scheme of golds and greens to harmonize with the colors of the green marble floors of the sanctuary. The designs incorporate the letter "M" and the fleur-de-lis flower of the Virgin.

The designs for the Chapel of the Resurrection are planned to harmonize with the glass mosaics in the reredos. The main theme is the blue of heaven and the golden circles of eternity. The colors are gold, aquamarine blue, rusty red, beige, and brown. The designs of the communion rail kneelers are of golden circles with red crosses in the center. The symbols of the phoenix, the butterfly, the lamb, and the dove are also enclosed in golden circles on other pieces for kneelers, stall cushions, and a Bishop's confirmation chair.

Red backgrounds, with designs of a center cross and background designs of fleur-de-lis, birds, grapes, and other motifs from nature—worked in red and gold and blues—form the motif for the needlepoint of Bethlehem Chapel.

In the Holy Spirit Chapel the needlework symbolism includes designs of the cross, the dove, and other symbols, against a background of grapes, all worked in tones of purple, white, and gold against a background color of robin's egg blue. One of the most interesting projects is the needlepoint being made for the Children's Chapel. The theme of these designs is the Noah's Ark story. The altar kneelers are long cushions. These tell the story of Noah and the Flood from the present-day child's point of view. On one long cushion are the Ark, the dove with olive branch, and the various kinds of wild animals. On another cushion are children at play with lambs and toys. The center cushion has a cross with lilies in its center and a kneeling angel to each side.

There are thirty small kneeling cushions. Each of these has a design of a single animal worked in its center—a lamb, a dog, a peacock, a sea gull, a dolphin, a rainbow trout, the eagle, the donkey, and many other wild and domesticated animals.

The long altar kneelers have a madonna blue background with a darker blue border. The animals and trees are in natural color and the Ark is in brown tones. The cushion with lilies has gold crosses and blonde angels in pink robes. The children in the other long cushion are worked in blues, reds, golds, and greens. The thirty small kneelers have a dark blue background and a gold border. The animals and birds are in natural colors, such as the striped rainbow trout. These cushions were all designed by Mrs. Fred Gurley of Winnetka, Illinois, together with Miss Dorothy Douville, and worked by Mrs. Gurley and her committee of twenty women.

With the great growth in the program of Christian education and the many new churches throughout the country with new children's chapels, this chapel offers a novel idea for decoration that might be used in other churches. There are many other popular and well-known Bible stories that could also be adapted for needlework, such as Joseph and the Coat of Many Colors, Jonah and the Whale, and the beautiful Christmas story of the Birth of Christ. Simple, clear-cut, direct designs and bright, clear colors appeal to children.

The shape, size, and purpose of church embroidery and needlepoint is mainly determined by tradition. The fitness of the design and the color, also, must harmonize with the service itself. Position and architectural backgrounds such as the color of the walls, stone, windows, and other decorations are also factors in the color and design of needlework for the church. Especially does this determine the dominant color of the needlework. Lighting must also be considered so that the needlework will show to good advantage.

The colors of church symbols and insignia are dictated by traditional usage, and thus harmonize with other liturgical furnishings as well as with old stained glass which follows tradition in its color usage.

Designs suitable for church usage include the symbols of the saints and the apostles, the insignia of the church and the insignia of state or diocese, which are similar to old heraldry designs used in English church decoration. Flowers of the Bible make particularly beautiful needlework designs. In fact even biblical scenes such as Daniel in the Lions' Den or Noah's Ark, which adapt themselves to conventional treatment, can be used. Of course subject matter with animals and figures is much more difficult to work and requires more skilled workmanship.

In past ages royal and noble ladies employed their leisure working embroidery or petit point for the adornment of churches and chapels. Cloths of gold or silver, and linen, wool, and silk materials were enriched with embroidery. The walls were "arrayed for a solemn feast with needlework made by our highborn ladies." There were also copes, chasubles, altar dossals and frontals, missal cushions, burses, veils, stoles, palls, and even rugs to be made and decorated. Anne of Brittany had her own workshop, and Isabella, sister of Louis XI, organized groups of women to work for the church. An embroiderer's

One of a pair of kneelers for the altar of St. John's Chapel, National Cathedral, Episcopal, Washington, D. C. On a scarlet background, the symbols are worked in gray and gold and greens, with bandings of gold. Design by Erica Wilson.

company was organized by Queen Elizabeth I.

In old wills and inventories there are numerous lists of embroidered vestments, hangings, frontals, and other ornaments of the church. Copes, carpets, and altar frontals were made not only with the emblems of the saints, but also with heraldic shields and the arms of Kings of England and lesser nobility. There were "curtains of red embroidered with white roses and the crossed keys of St. Peter"; there were albs and amices of linen "with orphreys of red velvet powdered and worked with little angels and the arms of England"; "a cope of red velvet with gold leopards and a border of blue velvet, woven with gold fleurs-de-lis"; and "a frontal with the arms of England and France in red and blue velvet woven with golden leopards and fleur-de-lis." Carpets of needlepoint were made of squares with flowers and with the bishop's insignia in a center square and the donor's coat of arms in the corners.

From old church inventories we have descriptions of carpets laid before the altar and on the choir and sanctuary pavements. Many are secular in design—"roses and stars in red, white, blue, and yellow"; "two large red carpets, one with arms of Lord Scrope"; "white carpet with double roses"; "blue carpets with arms"; "red carpet with leopards; blue with parrots; 2 yellow with parrots and roses"; "two large footcloths woven with lions to be laid before altars at great festivals"; "2 shorter ones trailed all over with flowers, for feast days of apostles."

Carpets for the altar steps or footpace made of wool on hemp are mentioned in inventories of Spanish churches—"red ground pattern of boughs and flowers in blue and the pomegranate"; "blue rug with yellow flower border and border of bar stripes of blue, yellow, and red—3 feet 10 inches by 3 feet 7 inches"; "dark blue pomegranate design on light blue spotted with crimson and white flower-like circles."

There are many books helpful in the design of church needlepoint. Those giving information on symbolism include *Church Symbolism* by F. R. Webber; *Signs and Symbols in Christian Art* by George Ferguson; *Glossary of Ecclesiastical Ornament* by A. Wilby Pugin; *Heraldry for Craftsmen and Designers* by Witt St. John Hope; and *The Sign Language of Our Faith* by Helen Stuart Griffith. There is also a wealth of design in the

Kneeler designed and embroidered by Ann Gillie for Guildford Cathedral, Surrey, England. One of sixty designs made or approved by the architect Sir Edward Maufe, R.A.

Noah's Ark design of large needlework cushion in the Children's Chapel, National Cathedral, Episcopal, Washington, D. C.

borders and medallions of old stained glass windows and in the wood carving of Gothic choir stalls and pew ends. Old pavement tiles and heraldic embroideries also offer a source of design for present-day church needlepoint and embroidery. However, church needlework need not be confined to old designs. Original, modern designs are also effective. The needlepoint kneelers being made for the Guildford Cathedral, Diocese of Guildford, England, are of modern design. Each kneeler is so arranged that the background is divided in half, one half representing the hill on which the cathedral is built, the other half the sky. The different designs are worked on this background. Other churches in England with recently completed needlework are Winchester Cathedral, Chelsea Old Church, and the Guards' Chapel, Wellington Barracks. The designs in the Guards' Chapel are badges of the different regiments worked on a blue ground. All these designs were prepared by the Royal School of Needlework, and I am indebted to Mrs. Hamilton-King, Principal, for the above information.

The Bethlehem Lutheran Church of Brooklyn owns a needlepoint superfrontal worked by the late King Gustav V of Sweden, which he pre-

sented to the church. It is a simple zig-zag design with a center IHS motif.

As more and more needlepoint is being made for the altars of American churches it is to be hoped that American scenes will be introduced into the designs. A city church might have symbolic designs set on a background of modern skyscrapers, a Midwestern church could use the prairie or the desert as a background, while the waves of the ocean would make a suitable background for needlework in seacoast churches. Although needlepoint is a traditional art and recalls the Gothic, it can be made in contemporary designs and can give the bit of color and enrichment so painfully needed in the new churches of the present day.

Flags and banners have been used in church processions and have been hung in churches on special occasions for many centuries. Many of the old flags and banners were painted and embroidered and some were appliquéd in simple banner designs. In the nineteenth century, embroidered banners became fancy and ornate and most of them were in such bad taste that it is too bad that they or their counterparts are to be seen in some churches today. There is nothing decorative about the average banner hung on a standard no matter how fine the stitchery. In fact, we would like to throw out the banner idea altogether with exception of a few examples, namely, those at Trinity Church, New York City, and those in the chapel of the Brick Presbyterian Church, New York City.

The banners at Trinity Church were designed for the enrichment of the church on the 250th anniversary of the founding of Trinity Parish. There are twenty-nine banners representing insignia of churches, chapels, and institutions founded or aided by Trinity Church. These are in striking colors and simple designs appliquéd on rectangular banners. Many of the banners were designed by Thomas M. Bell, architect, and the Reverend Dr. Edward N. West, Canon Sacrist of the Cathedral of St. John the Divine, New York City.

Another excellent example of the use of banners in church decoration is to be seen in the chapel of Brick Presbyterian Church. These banners represent the great Synods of the Presbyterian Church.

Needlepoint cushion designed by the Misses Tebbetts Needlepoint Studio, and worked by Mrs. Ralph Matthiesen for one of the choir stalls of the National Cathedral, Episcopal, Washington, D. C.

11

The Church Organ as Decoration
The Choir and Choir Vestry

*I*N designing a new church, the architect must provide adequate space for the organ. That space should be a part of the architectural plan of the church—not an afterthought.

At one time the organ was the dominant feature of the church. Organ cases often cost as much as organs. They were constructed in the same style as the building and its furnishings. There were Gothic organ cases with pinnacles, crockets, and finials, with intricate carved figures of the Virgin and angels, in the niches. Decorated shutters were made to close and protect the organ pipes. The pipes themselves were painted with gold and polychrome. Fine old Gothic cases are still to be seen, especially in Spain.

Italian Renaissance organ cases were square, architectural forms topped with a pediment. They were also completely covered with ornament and polychrome decoration. The French organs had heavily carved baroque and Louis Quinze rococo cases. Some of the most fantastic cases were made in Germany and Holland. In England one of the most interesting old organ cases is in King's College, Cambridge. This Renaissance case is topped with crowns, arms, and Tudor badges.

There are a few examples of old organ cases in America. The most interesting is in Trinity Lutheran Church at Lancaster, Pennsylvania. The old organ and case of Colonial design were built in 1774. Although the organ was rebuilt in 1923, the case remains as it was originally designed. Another example is the carved baroque case of the Methuen Memorial Music Hall organ at Methuen, Massachusetts.

A nineteenth-century example of a large organ case is in the Mormon Tabernacle in Salt Lake City. The organ case is set out in the auditorium and has the outline of a turreted castle.

The organ pipes are the main feature of the chapel at the United States Naval Academy at Annapolis, Maryland. The organ cases seem to be a part of the architecture of the building. They are placed at the sides of the chancel and do not usurp the space of the altar. The gold colored pipes are also a part of the gold and white and blue color scheme of the chapel. The setting of the pipes blends with the architectural form as well as with the decorative scheme.

Grace Episcopal Church, New York City, designed in the earlier nineteenth century by James Renwick, has gilt and polychrome pipes exposed to view in a case at the side of the chancel and also a carved wooden case resembling a Gothic cathedral that houses the pipes over the gallery. It is a relic of another day.

In the nineteenth century, the organ pipes and their cases were often given the space at the eastern end of the church and placed there without any regard for the basic architecture of the church. The church was designed, then the organ was installed, and a superstructure was built about the pipes. The result was an overpowering, ugly structure that dominated the church interior.

In the liturgical church, the organ pipes were usually put to the sides of the chancel or at the back of the church, for the altar occupied the space at the eastern end. In the Union Theological Seminary, New York City, the organ pipes are

105

Exposed organ pipes and Gothic carved tracery, Christ Church Cathedral, Episcopal, Indianapolis, Indiana. M. P. Möller, Inc.

in plain view, placed and grouped so that their tubular forms repeat the design of the columns supporting the Gothic vaulting.

The organ pipes and case in the Gothic chapel at Washington University, St. Louis, Missouri, become a part of the dark and light architectural pattern. There is also a beautiful organ case in the Church of St. James the Less, Philadelphia.

The organ pipes in the Protestant Chapel at the United States Military Academy at West Point, New York, and in the Chapel of the Intercession, New York City, designed by Bertram Goodhue, are exposed to view at the side of the chancel. They are an integral part of the architecture.

However, not all architects can handle the problem of the exposed organ pipes, and within the last fifty years the general tendency has been to hide the pipes from view. Organs were put in chambers and thus incorporated in the building. They did not need cases. This is acoustically bad, for the organ should be heard first and seen second. It is far better to spend money for more pipes than for a case or elaborate screen. An exposed organ gives better sound.

There have been screens of all types and styles. There have been beautiful lacework Gothic screens and there have been intricately carved wooden screens. In the old Emmanuel Church, Boston, Massachusetts, there is a combination of organ pipes and screens skillfully designed. But the majority of the nineteenth-century and early twentieth-century treatments have been just ugly screens placed over a hole in the wall, behind which stood the organ pipes, their beautiful tubular forms of tin, copper, spotted metal, or wood more decorative than the screens which concealed them from view.

The elaborately perforated organ screen designed by Eliel and Eero Saarinen for the Tabernacle Church of Christ at Columbus, Indiana, set the pattern for new and attractive organ settings. Sheet music of favorite hymns, perfectly scaled in bronze, forms the unique organ grilles on either side of the choir in the Bertha E. R. Strosacker Memorial Presbyterian Church, Midland, Michigan. In the First Congregational Church, Berkeley, California, the dark rectangular organ grilles are spaced to enhance the architectural lines and make a pleasing contrast of dark tone in the light walls. These are only a few examples of organ screens that are being designed so that they add to the decoration of the church.

However, new functional designers are interested in the functionally exposed organ pipes. Indeed, those familiar with the background of the pipe organ and its traditional use in the church seem to agree that it is proper and fitting to see the organ pipes.

A dramatic placement of organ pipes is seen in the chapel designed by Eero Saarinen for Massachusetts Institute of Technology. The design of the organ pipes in the modern Kruiskerk in Amsterdam repeats the angles of the church architecture. When the organ of St. Bartholomew's Church, New York City, was rebuilt in 1953, the pipes were exposed, and the pipes of mahogany, tin, copper, and spotted metal blend unobtrusively with the rich mosaics and colored marble.

Those who build organs have long known that the best sound cannot come from an instrument buried within the church walls. Thus they welcome the use of functionally exposed pipes.

In planning a new church or in alterations of an existing building, the organ builder as well as the architect should be consulted as soon as possible for a saving of both time and money. An organ is bought once in a lifetime, and the best expert advice is necessary to avoid mistakes. The expert organ builder studies the intended home of the organ and consults not only the architect, but also the organist and those concerned with the musical program.

The size of the organ is determined by the over-all size of the church. For a very large church, a four-manual pipe organ is required. A smaller church will require a three- or a two-manual organ. The organ is designed specifically for the church which it is to occupy. Organs not only have case styles to harmonize with buildings of classic, baroque, romantic, or Renaissance architecture, but the organ itself has an individual personality. No two organs are alike. Every pipe organ, whether three centuries old or built today, is designed and built as an individual instrument. From the musical standpoint, an organ may be baroque, classical, romantic, or Renais-

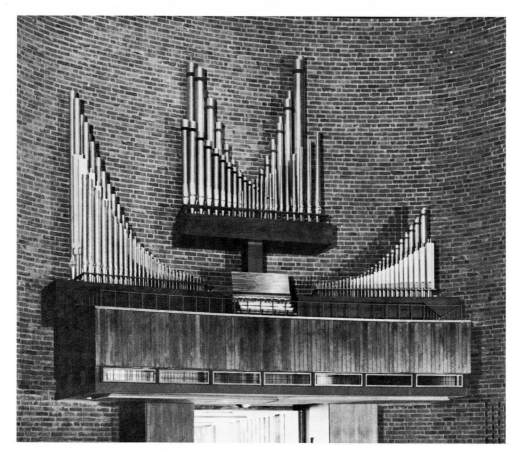

Exposed organ pipes in Chapel at the Massachusetts Institute of Technology, Cambridge, Massachusetts. Designed by Walter Holtkamp.

sance. There are also national and denominational variations. Traditionally, organs have been tailored to the ritual and taste of individual congregations and specific organists and composers. Older organs, like old buildings, are composite edifices, with sections dating from different periods.

Before discarding an old organ, several experts should be called in. Many churches have fine old pipe organs which need only reconditioning. If a church has been enlarged so that the present organ no longer fits the building, consideration should be given to the enlargement of the organ chamber. It will also be necessary to increase the volume and melodic versatility. Old organs and old buildings both give off mellow melodies.

So closely is the organ and its building interwoven that an organ moved from one location to another must be rebuilt before it can sound its best in its new acoustical surroundings.

Today many fine organs are being built, or re-

built, after old traditions. The interest in old organs springs from the revival of old music. Thus a present-day organ may be based on a classic foundation—the eighteenth-century organ—which had great tone richness, clarity, and brilliance. To this will be added the best modern developments in tone and mechanical facility.

From the sound standpoint, the organ should be placed where it can give the best musical effectiveness. If the pipes are to be concealed, they should not be hidden by structural materials that will muffle or distort the organ tone, but by materials that will have a maximum sound conductivity. An organ needs good air circulation. A shallow chamber of great height and width is the best space for the organ. If all divisions of the organ are on the same level, it is easier to tune the organ. The walls about the organ should be smooth plaster or hard wood so that no particles will fall on the organ pipes. An organ is also designed in accordance with the music it will be required to play.

A superb organ is good even in unfavorable surroundings, but the organ is at its best in the proper acoustical environment. Even temperature and good air circulation cut down the cost of frequent tuning.

The best location for the major part of the organ is in front of a solid wall. The organ console should not be so close to the pipes that the organist hears only the organ and not the choir. The organist should also see the choir without using a mirror. The ideal setup is to locate the choir in front of the organ and the console in front of the choir stalls.

Electronic organs are usually less expensive than pipe organs. A church with limited space can accommodate an electric organ better than a pipe organ. An electronic organ also requires less upkeep. For these reasons many new, small and medium sized churches are installing electronic organs.

Although much may be said in favor of the electronic organ, it was originally invented for the music hall rather than the church. As a church instrument it has not reached its full development. It will take years of experiment and study before the electronic organ will compare with the individual hand-crafted organ for church use.

Whatever type of organ you plan for your church, there must also be a choir. The position of the choir is of utmost importance. Will the choir be in the chancel at the front of the church, or will the organ and choir be placed in the balcony over the church narthex? The position of the choir will depend in part upon the denomination

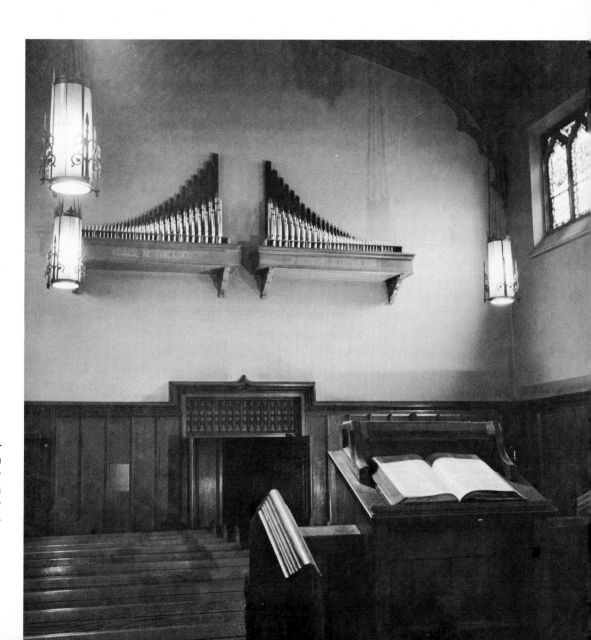

Holmes Chapel, Westminster Presbyterian Church, Buffalo, New York. Exposed organ pipes add to the dignity of the setting. Aeolian-Skinner Organ Co.

of the church. The Roman Catholic Church places the choir and the organ at the back of the church. Also the size of the church and the size of the choir influence the position of the choir. If a shallow chancel is planned, there may not be space for the choir in that location.

The placing of the choir must of course be decided upon before the architect is called in to design the church and before the organ designer is asked to design and build the organ. The placing of the choir influences the location of the organ. If the choir is in the gallery, the organ should be there too. Wherever the choir is placed, there must be appropriate seats and adequate lighting.

In addition to the space in the church itself, the choir will need a room for rehearsal and for the storage of vestments. This room is usually called the choir vestry. The choir vestry should be situated so that the choir can form for the processional. In a church which does not have a proces-

sional, the requirements of the choir vestry are the same, but the location is not so important. It should be a large-sized room. The room should include cabinets for music storage and lockers for choir vestments. There should be a piano, a clock, and benches arranged choir-wise. With so much storage space and locker room, a wood-panelled room is the result and this makes for a good-looking room as well. The vestry or practice room should also have good acoustics and adequate light.

In this chapter the discussion has purposely been confined to the appearance and location of the organ and the choir and their part in the decorative and architectural scheme of the church. Any recommendations as to the music of the church and the musical performance of the organ should be answered by experts in that field.

The majesty, beauty, and serenity characteristic of organ tone are conducive to many facets of the Worship of Almighty God, whether the medium be one of repentance, supplication, adoration, praise, or thanksgiving. Ecclesiastical Music is not only an inspirational element in Divine Worship, but has brought hope, courage, solace, increased devotion, and renewed faith to countless Christians; the effectiveness of which has been greatly intensified through the transcendental beauty of the organ. No other instrument can lead the congregation's participation in the singing of hymns; accompany the choir in the musical portions of the Liturgy; and permeate an edifice with an aura of spiritual devotion more compellingly yet unobtrusively than the organ.

—From Notes describing the organs at Grace Cathedral, San Francisco

Bertha E. R. Strosacker Memorial Presbyterian Church, Midland, Michigan. The organ screens are hymns executed in gold and silver Alumilited aluminum, with adjustable louvers in back. Edward Coe Embury and Aymar Embury II, architects.

12

The Sacristies and The Minister's Study

*E*very liturgical church should have two sacristies—one for the clergy and one for the Altar Guild. The latter is called the working sacristy. Both of these sacristies should be near the chancel, and the clergy's sacristy should open out onto the chancel if possible.

The working sacristy should be large and convenient for efficient work. There should be cupboards and drawers for altar linens, vestments, candles, vases, and other appointments for the services. If altar frontals and dossals are used, the room should be large enough to hold cases or cupboards to hang these without folding.

There are two special functions of the working sacristy, first of all the care and preparation of the altars and baptismal font for services. There should be drawers for altar linens and burses and veils and cabinets for keeping the vested chalice. There should be a small safe for the communion vessels, the wine, and the wafers. Altar vases, alms basins, processional crosses, altar candles, and censers should all be stored and cared for in the working sacristy. If possible there should be a piscina, or drain, for disposing of water left from the altar and font. (See *Good Housekeeping in the Church* by Katharine Morrison McClinton and Isabel Wright Squier.)

For the necessary work in preparing and cleaning vessels and linens, there should be a sink and drainboard and a folding ironing board. A large table is the best working space for vesting the chalice. This should be conveniently placed near the clean linens and chalice vestments. An ample sized closet is necessary for workers' coats and hats and altar guild uniforms, as well as for space for storage of pressed and unpressed vestments.

The working sacristy also serves as the flower arrangement room. In a non-liturgical church, the working sacristy may be smaller, because there is less work to be done. There will, however, need to be space for arranging flowers and for the communion vessels that are used.

The working sacristy should not have the appearance of a kitchen, but should have dignity of appearance. For this reason, its walls and general decoration should be the same as the church proper. There may be simple casements, cloth draperies at the windows, and a cross or crucifix over the piscina to suggest the high purpose of the room.

Vestment drawers in the priest's sacristy of the Church of the Heavenly Rest, New York City.

Working sacristy of the Church of the Heavenly Rest, New York City.

The clergy's sacristy is the room where the priest vests himself for the service. It should contain closets for robes and vestments when not in use. If it is necessary for the acolytes to use the same room, their vestments must be kept in extra closets for that purpose. However, if possible there should be a separate room for the acolytes, or they may use the same room as the choir. The clergy's sacristy should have an adjoining toilet and wash room. The clergy's sacristy should also include a vesting case with drawers for vestments prepared for the services and extra drawers for stoles, girdles, amices, and other articles of clerical dress. The vested chalice may be set on the top of this case prior to being carried to the communion service.

The clergy's sacristy should connect with the minister's study so that he can enter without going out into a hallway. There should also be a doorway leading to the chancel.

From the standpoint of decoration the room should be simple and dignified. A cross or crucifix may be placed over the vestment case. A simple floor covering and draperies are desirable to give the room dignity. A large table to hold the church record book is needed as well as a small bookcase, or book shelves, for extra Bibles, prayer books, and hymn books. While the room should be neatly furnished, order, dignity, and cleanliness are more important than decoration. Floor coverings of asphalt tile would be suitable and easy to keep clean. In the non-liturgical church the clergy's sacristy will not be needed. A study, with wardrobe, toilet, and wash room facilities is required in churches of all denominations.

The minister's study should be near the east entrance to the church. It should have an adjoining secretary's office and reception room, if possible, and should also have a direct connection with the chancel of the church. The minister's study must serve several purposes. It must be convenient and efficient for work. There must be file cases for his records. There should be a bookcase for reference. A clock is a necessity and should be in plain view on the wall, on a mantel or on a bookcase, or on his desk or writing table.

The minister also receives persons making plans for a baptism, a wedding, or a funeral. It is in his office that he consults those in need of advice and gives solace to those in trouble. For

112

these purposes the minister's study should be comfortable, attractive, and dignified. There should be easy chairs, good light, an open fireplace when possible, and pleasing decoration. Finally, the minister uses his study for writing his sermons. For this purpose there should be adequate light from windows and also satisfactory artificial lighting. For inspiration there may be a cross or crucifix, a fine piece of sculpture, or a religious picture. Where possible, a distant view or a door opening on a garden would give an inspirational break.

Now given all this framework of necessary elements, how should the minister's study be furnished? With dignified comfortable furniture of a style that fits the general scheme of the church decoration. The colors will be decided by the size of the room and the exposure, but they should be cheerful and not too light. The room should be masculine.

Where possible, a general plan of decoration for the administration and social wing of the church, which may or may not include the minister's study, should be made. One style of furniture may be decided upon and the colors of rooms may be chosen so that they harmonize. One wall color can be chosen for all, but the

rooms can be given individual character by means of accent of different colors in each room. The decorations of the rooms of the Bertha E. R. Strosacker Memorial Presbyterian Church in Midland, Michigan, are an interesting example.

The church itself is a beautiful example of American Georgian, with unique detailed ornament of exterior and interior which combines traditional and new materials. The furniture follows the style of the architecture. In this church the furniture and decorations in the various areas of the church are a complete cross section of regional furnishings in Federal American—from the dignity of metropolitan decorations in the parlor and reception room to the various types of American provincial in the less formal rooms of the Sunday school, Fellowship room, and library.

In a church of contemporary design, the furniture and decoration in the administrative and social rooms will want to be in the same general style as the church. But the fads and extremes of modern decoration do not belong in church buildings. No matter what style the church decoration may be, good, simple furniture of strong construction, materials of lasting quality, and a pleasing color scheme should be chosen. A certain amount of dignity and formality should also characterize church or parish house furnishings.

Architect's drawing of First Methodist Church, Niles, Ohio. Harold E. Wagoner and Donald L. Bostwick, architects.

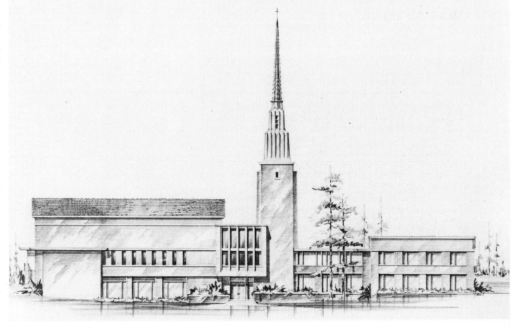

13

The Church Social Center

THE ideal social setup of the church should include a ladies' parlor, an auditorium or assembly room, a kitchen, a library, and a bride's dressing room. The position of these rooms will depend on the particular arrangement. All of these rooms, plus the Sunday school, may be in one building connected with the church proper by a cloister. Another plan is to have the offices and social center in one building and the Sunday school in a separate building. The plan of such physical layouts can be determined by the minister and building committee, with the aid of the architect.

The ladies' parlor should be the size of a large living room. Twenty by thirty feet is a good size. This room will be used for committee meetings and for small gatherings. It can be used as a waiting room if near the minister's office. If the ladies' parlor adjoins the assembly room, it will serve as a place to set up the table for the coffee hour after church.

The ladies' parlor should be furnished as any attractive living room. It should have plenty of windows, a fireplace, bookcases, a large table with magazines, and comfortable chairs and sofas. The furniture style should follow the style of the church, although when we say style we do not mean an old-fashioned period room. We mean Georgian type furniture in a Georgian church and contemporary furniture in a contemporary church. In most churches this room will also double as the library. For this reason one wall might be given over to bookcases, where there will be books on subjects related to the church. There should not only be religious books, but books of general interest, such as books on the cathedrals of Europe, stained glass, and sculpture. The colors used in the decoration of the ladies' parlor will be determined by the exposure and size of the room. The floor covering may be carpeting or some resilient such as asphalt tile or cork.

Here are some sample color schemes.

For a light room:
    Walls—gray-green
    Rug—darker gray-green
    Draperies—green and white and deep pink pattern linen chintz
    Upholstery—sofa: brown; chairs: white, green, dusty pink, and brown stripes; side chairs: dusty pink leather

For a dark room:
    Walls—creamy yellow
    Rug or floor—green

One of the rooms in the parish house of Trinity Church, New York City. The movable partitions make the room flexible so that it can be used as a large dining room, a chapel, or Sunday school rooms.

The library of the First Baptist Church, Greensboro, North Carolina, has early American furniture reproductions, an asbestos tile floor, and ample bookshelves. Albert C. Woodroof and Eggers & Higgins, architects.

Draperies—red and green chintz
Upholstery—sofa: green; chairs: red and green chintz; side chairs: yellow and green stripes.

There should be a rest room adjoining the ladies' parlor.

The bride's dressing room may be combined with the ladies' rest rooms or it may be a separate room. The room should be convenient to the church proper, so that it is not necessary to go outside to enter the church. It should be large enough for at least a dozen persons to occupy at the same time. It should include a dressing table with a three way mirror and also a full-length wall mirror. There should be seats for at least a half dozen persons. Benches attached to the walls are excellent as seating furniture here. There should be an adjoining lavatory.

The decoration of the bride's room should be gay and attractive. Light colored chintzes of floral design are appropriate. The walls could be papered or hung with floral prints. The floors can be of asphalt tile, which is easy to keep clean.

The lighting is important, and if there are no windows the artificial lighting should be planned to concentrate on the mirrors. After all, in most churches, weddings are a source of revenue to the church as well as the minister, so that it is good thinking to plan for facilities that make the bride and her attendants comfortable. It must be disappointing to arrive at the church and not find a mirror for one last full-length look at your gown and veil before you start up the aisle. There are often emergencies and last-minute adjustments necessary to the gowns of the bride and her attendants.

The assembly room may double as an auditorium. It should be large enough to seat from one hundred to five hundred people, according to the size of the congregation. It will be used for large meetings, for the church sewing groups, and as a dining room for church breakfasts, luncheons, and suppers. It should be equipped with folding chairs and folding tables. A stage for church plays and pageants and a screen for church movies is also desirable. From the decorative standpoint,

Bertha E. R. Strosacker Memorial Presbyterian Church, Midland, Michigan. The assembly room with stage and group of upholstered furniture for small group meetings. Bennetts Inc., decorators. Edward Coe Embury and Aymar Embury II, architects.

the room should be simple and dignified. Heavy materials at the windows should hang floor length to match the stage curtains. If the room adjoins the ladies' parlor, it will need no other furniture. If it is a separate room, it might be well to have a grouping of upholstered furniture to serve as a nucleus for a discussion group. The stage can also double as a committee meeting room. The chairs and tables of the assembly room can be stored under the stage. If the panel is removed in the space beneath the stage, the chairs and tables may easily be put in without the inconvenience of using corridors or stairways.

Adjoining the auditorium or assembly room should be a kitchen. The modern kitchen in a large present-day church should be geared for both cafeteria and table service. For large church dinners of 150 or more, table service is more efficient. For smaller gatherings, cafeteria service is more desirable and less costly. To provide a suitable kitchen for your particular church, the building committee should make a careful study of the present and future demands. The women who have planned and served church suppers should be consulted. Also if there is someone in the parish in the electrical or kitchen equipment

business it is well to get their interest and advice at the planning stage. Then the resulting survey should be talked over with the architect, who will gather information from the kitchen equipment companies. Installations of electric wiring and gas piping should anticipate future as well as present kitchen requirements. Most public utility companies would be glad to volunteer suggestions on plumbing and wiring. This will prevent needless future expense.

A single oven is no longer sufficient for the church kitchen. In addition, there should be a smooth-top stove with oven and broiler and perhaps an extra bake oven. The large church that serves four to five hundred people at its church suppers requires heavy duty hotel ranges and roasting ovens, together with separate bake ovens. The cafeteria counter will need to have about fifty feet of serving space with steam tables and cold unit. There should be cupboards below and above. The counter should be stainless steel. A water cooler and a coffee urn of stainless steel are also desirable.

Electric equipment of a large church kitchen will include electric mixers, hot plates, toasters, and a potato peeler. A refrigerator with a freez-

Bishop Tuttle Memorial, Episcopal, St. Louis, Missouri. Food service counter. Designed by Frank G. Hilliker and Associates, Food Service Consultants.

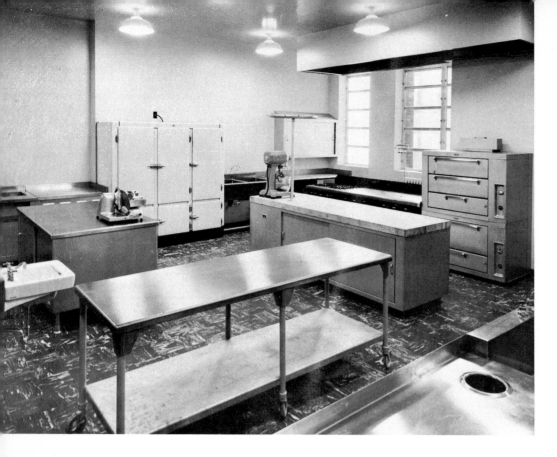

ing compartment will be large enough for the small church, but a large church could use a separate freezer.

A dishwasher is a must in the church kitchen. It should be surrounded by ample counter space for soiled dishes and at least two sinks for scraping and cleaning. On the other side of the dishwasher there should be drying racks for the clean dishes. A garbage disposal unit is also desirable and an incinerator for other waste. Naturally, if these are not possible, ample garbage and waste cans are needed.

Of course the kitchen equipment includes all sizes of pots and pans, a meat grinder, knives and forks and spoons, cannisters, waste baskets, brooms and mops, as well as such individual items as a can opener and a bottle opener. There should be ample wall cabinets to store all these items. Separate cabinets for dishes and glassware should be nearer the serving center. There must be storage for linens, china, and silver. An extra room for the storage of food is desirable. This should be large enough to store cases of canned goods.

Rolling pickup trucks are needed to transport food when table service is used and to return dirty dishes from the tables to the kitchen.

It is important that the kitchen have proper ventilation, so that smoke, heat, and cooking odors will not fill the dining area. An electric fan in the stove hood will be satisfactory. If there are no windows for fresh air, some kind of a ventilating system is needed.

The whole kitchen setup should be planned not only with efficient equipment, but with permanent backgrounds such as tiled walls, which can hold a mosaic or decorative tile panel. Stainless steel stoves and other equipment and formica counters need less labor, and since the women in most churches do the work, these things are a must.

An attractive color scheme in all kitchen backgrounds, as well as in dishes, will add to its efficient appearance. If the walls are not of ceramic tile, they should at least be of some washable material such as wall linoleum. The floor of course should be linoleum, vinyl tile, or greaseproof asphalt tile. Tile may form a wainscot reaching a height to cover all wall space that might get greasy food spots. The wall above the wainscot should be hard plaster painted with an enamel finish. This painted surface may be a contrasting color to the tile. A tile wainscot with a panel inset of fruit or vegetables would be attractive. The wall might also be a tile pattern of loaves and fishes (see cover of author's *Loaves and Fishes*). The design might be carried out in light and dark blue, with a rust red linoleum floor. Gray and yellow, with a blue linoleum floor, makes an attractive kitchen; or you can use light and dark vermilion, with a bit of black, and a black floor. The colors should, however, harmonize with the adjoining room. The kitchen should have plenty of light from the right size fluorescent fixtures. There should not only be a central fixture, but there should be supplementary fixtures at the range, sink, and refrigerator.

There should be good planning when kitchens are to be set up for mass feeding. Basic positioning of the pieces of equipment in relation to each other is necessary to prevent waste of time, labor, money, even dishes and food. Think through the number of people involved; the time element (for serving); the menu (limited or diversified); and the seating capacity of your room (in order to arrange for best flow of cooking and serving).

Use common sense in the arrangement. Try to get a minimum of handling and transporting of unprepared food, prepared food, and dishes—before and after washing. Avoid cross-over of traffic, and locate equipment at point of most frequent use.

A kitchen plan should be based on steps and routes taken in food preparation. Thus you will find that the plan of an efficient kitchen is best when the equipment and cabinets form a "U" in a continuous line around three sides of a kitchen. The kitchen equipment is then based around the three centers—the refrigerator, the sink, and the range.

The refrigerator center is also the space where the food is prepared. The refrigerator stores the perishable food, and the canned foods, flour, sugar, spices, all the bowls for preparing the food, the pans for cooking the food, and the mixers and other implements used in cooking should be stored in the space near the refrigerator.

The sink and dishwasher area should include the sinks, dishwasher, disposal unit, and all the

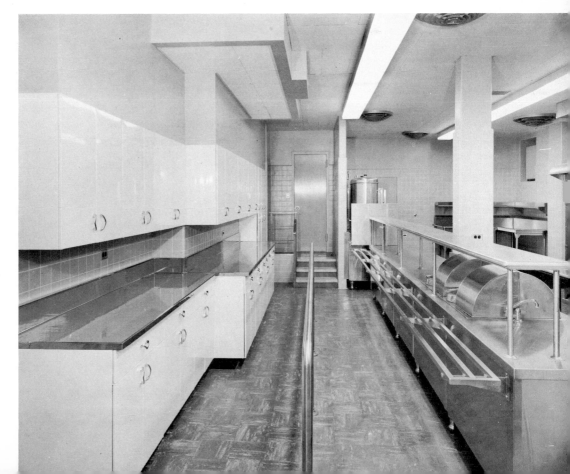

Madison Avenue Presbyterian Church, New York City. Cafeteria and dish storage area of parish house. Equipment furnished by Straus-Duparquet, Inc. Thos. Bell, architect.

soaps, cleansers, and brushes used. The dish storage cabinets should be near by.

The range and serving center includes the stove, pots and pans for cooking, and dishes for serving. For greatest convenience, the sink should be between the refrigerator and the range center. In the open cafeteria-type kitchen, the counter occupies the fourth side of the kitchen. When the kitchen is planned in connection with a combination assembly hall dining room, there should be a folding partition that can completely shut off the kitchen when not in use.

The "cafe" type range, a steam table, a mobile serving unit, and a two-bowl sink will serve as minimum, but adequate, equipment for the average church. Of course it is possible to serve a church dinner without all this elaborate equipment. However, in these days of labor-scarcity it is well to have electric devices and equipment for self-service. Also the present-day social program of the church make the parish house or social center an important functional part of the church organization.

Suggested color schemes for church dining rooms:

1. Lime yellow walls; deep blue asphalt tile floor; draperies with floral pattern of blue, yellows, orange, and greens.

2. Platinum gray walls; bone white ceiling; red tile floor; draperies and wall decorations of red, gray, and yellow.

Madison Avenue Presbyterian Church, New York City. Cooking and serving area of parish house. Equipment furnished by Straus-Duparquet, Inc. Thos. Bell, architect.

120

14

Planning for the Church School

In BOTH new and old present-day congregations, one of the most important building problems is the creation of adequate church school space. Most churches need more church school space than they can afford. Not only must the church provide space for their present Sunday school enrollment, but they must allow for expansion. The size of the congregation will help decide the size of the church school needs. Generally speaking, the seating capacity of the church school should equal the seating capacity of the nave of the church. However, in suburban communities, where the tendency today is to have from three to five children per family, the church school enrollment may far outnumber the adult church attendance. An important fact to remember is that the growth of the church comes through the Sunday school. A growing Sunday school means a growing church—a dwindling Sunday school means a failing church. While ideal buildings and equipment do not make a Sunday school, they are a great help.

There are two solutions to the housing of the fast-growing church school. One is to have two separate sessions of the church school; the other is to have a flexible parish house plan. Flexible classroom partitions can be adjusted with change in size of the class and they can be moved back to create one large assembly room, thus making the space serve two purposes.

The changing church is nowhere more apparent than in the broadened scope of the Christian education program which includes many types of organizations and activities. It is extremely important that provision of space and equipment for educational purposes be commensurate with the scope and importance of the program.

The ultimate objective of the Christian educa-

tion program today is to produce mature Christian disciples. The achievement of this goal requires a wide variety of types of study, worship, recreation, creative activities, fellowship, and group projects—all included in the Christian education program. The Sunday school is only one of the organizations which promotes this program. There are also the weekday church school, youth organizations, graded choirs, the vacation school, scout groups, young adult groups, parent groups, and separate women's and men's associations.

The needs of the different educational groups are met more effectively when adequate buildings and equipment are provided. In undertaking a major building program, consideration must not only be given to present needs, but the changing needs of the future must be anticipated. This requires a survey not only of the church, but of the whole community. With the results of such a survey, the church is then ready to talk about space, equipment, and room requirements. Many churches have made such surveys, yet because of unforeseen changes in the community found that on the completion of their new building the space and equipment were inadequate. A flexible plan which makes use of multiple services and utilization of space will help such a situation.

Building plans, whether for the erection of a new building or for a remodeling project, should be determined by the program needs of a congregation. Many churches have made serious mistakes by plunging into building projects before making a careful study of the program and the kinds of building facilities and equipment needed in order to carry on their programs effectively, and the possibilities of multi-sessions for church services and church school as well as multi-purpose use of every area.

Bertha E. R. Strosacker Memorial Presbyterian Church, Midland, Michigan. The semicircular chancel or choir, in the center, is flanked on the left by the administrative offices, recreational and social wing, and on the right by the Sunday school and chapel. Edward Coe Embury and Aymar Embury II, architects.

Persons on building committees should become acquainted with present trends in Christian education that have important bearing on the kinds of building facilities required. Some of these tend to include freedom and flexibility in method, based on the principle that persons learn by doing. This calls for more space and larger rooms. Worship is now an integral part of class and department programs and is generally conducted in the department assembly room. Starting even with the kindergarten children, a worship service somewhat formal in nature is used. For older children, youth, and adults worship is conducted in the department rooms or a church chapel may be used. Another trend in Christian education is instruction in coeducational classes. This means larger classes and thus larger rooms, so that study group activity and worship may be conducted in the same room. If the department is large, it may be divided into grades and each grade have a separate room.

Christian education in the Church today has expanded from the old-fashioned Sunday school of ten or twenty years ago and has an increased importance in the church program. It is based on approved procedures and materials which aid in teaching Christian development. The programs recommended usually follow a plan of a class period, with good teachers and approved materials, and a worship period with departmental chapels or worship in a chapel with a minister. In addition, there are weekday fellowship activities which include social and sports activities, as well as drama and pageantry. A good Sunday school also has a program of visual education which includes the use of slides, filmstrips, and motion pictures. A library of selected books for all ages is also an important part of today's Christian education. However, the improved concepts of the educational program suggest emphasis on training for worship, rather than an attempt of the church to assert itself as a substitute for a community recreation center.

The church school is usually housed in a wing of the church or in the parish house, which may be connected to the church proper by a cloister. It may be housed in a one- or two-story building. The building should provide space for recreation as well as teaching and worship. When possible, the nursery and lower grades should be on the

Plainfield Methodist Church, Plainfield, Iowa. One of the Sunday school rooms, showing modern furniture and stools that stack when not in use. Schweikher and Elting, architects.

ground floor so that the small children can enter directly from the outside and not climb too many steps.

The rooms should be as light and attractive as possible, easy to maintain and consistent with the furnishings of the rest of the building. There should be plenty of windows and adequate artificial light for use when necessary. Halls, stairs, and doorways should be at least 5 feet wide, for safety. If a basement is to be used for classrooms, there should be adequate light and protection against dampness. Walls and floors must be waterproofed to prevent mildew, and the heating must keep the floors warm. When classrooms are formed by dividing assembly rooms with folding partitions, the partitions should reach the ceiling and be as soundproof as possible.

The present-day Sunday school is usually divided into departments, with an assembly room or chapel for each department and separate classes for small groups of each department. The exact divisions and age groups for which space must be provided will vary in different churches, but the departments most generally found are Nursery, Kindergarten or Beginners, Primary, Junior, Junior High or Intermediate, and Senior.

The Nursery department children will range from fifteen months to two or three years. This department should have one large room, with a smaller adjoining room furnished with cribs or playpens. The rooms should be light and the windows low enough for the children to see out. There should be shelves and cupboards for toys and furniture scaled to size. Coatroom facilities should also be scaled to small size. There should be a small sink and toilet facilities which can be shared with the Kindergarten. There should be low bulletin boards on the walls, and the floors should be of soft, durable, easy-to-clean material such as asphalt tile. The Nursery department should have a separate outside entrance if possible.

The Kindergarten should have furniture scaled to size and separate coatroom lockers. Different age groups should have different classrooms, with one large assembly room at least 30 by 40 feet in size. The size of course will vary with the individual church. Toilets and coatrooms should be provided. The walls may have blackboards, bulletin boards, and pictures. There should be a folding or movable altar, or worship center, in the group assembly room. The need of the individual

Sunday school will determine the size of the rooms. The Protestant International Council of Religious Education has a chart of recommended classroom sizes with the footage per pupil for each age group. Required equipment is also listed. The smaller children may have their chairs set about tables, but older children can have chairs arranged in aisles as in a church or chapel. Folding chairs and tables are not desirable.

The Primary Department should have a large assembly room with a folding altar, or worship center. The number of classrooms will depend upon the size of the enrollment, and the manner of distribution will depend on the instruction used in different denominations. Coatrooms and toilet facilities are important with this age group.

The Junior department should also have a general assembly room with a folding worship center and separate classrooms. If there is a chapel, the Juniors can share it with the Junior High or Intermediates, or can rotate the use of the chapel for separate services.

The Junior High, or, Intermediate, and the Senior classrooms should again be separate from the other departments. They should be made larger to accommodate more pupils in each room. They should use the church or chapel as their assembly room.

If a church school chapel is within the budget, it is desirable to use it beginning with the Junior age group. The chapel can be designed exactly the same as an adult chapel with altar, lectern, font, and pews. In some denominations the children read the scriptures, usher, and take the collection, as well as light the candles and have a children's choir. The Wilshire Methodist Church in Los Angeles has a children's chapel for children from six to twelve years of age. The chapel holds 125 children. The service is held from 11:00 to 12:15, at the same time the adults' church service is in session.

The New First Reformed Church of Pella, Iowa, has a children's chapel which is an exact replica of the adult's chapel.

In some denominations the chapel service is conducted by the minister in the church proper and classroom study follows.

When arranging a worship center, or a chapel for children, it is well to keep in mind the influence of attractive surroundings on the child's mind. If the child is to be taught to worship in an assembly room instead of a church or chapel, there should at least be a resemblance to a church. A formal treatment, such as rows of chairs or benches arranged with aisles as the pews in a church, is much more conducive to worship than

Bertha E. R. Strosacker Memorial Presbyterian Church, Midland, Michigan. The secondary, or junior, worship center. Edward Coe Embury and Aymar Embury II, architects.

chairs about a table. The altar, no matter how small, should have a cross and candlesticks and some decoration to give it emphasis. If possible, it should have flower vases with flowers, as in a church, or a dossal or a painted decoration on the triptych that folds to conceal the worship center when not in use. If a separate children's chapel is planned, it should not be bare of color and decoration. The children's chapel in St. John's Church, Sharon, Pennsylvania, has an altar with carved decoration, a dossal, and a beautiful stained glass window. Such a chapel would be a beautiful memorial gift in memory of a child.

Religious drama is now widely used as a technique of teaching religious education. Informal creative plays and play readings can be a part of the regular teaching program. This will not require a stage or an extra room, but will need costumes and properties and therefore a storage space should be provided for them. However, many churches produce only an occasional play, such as a Christmas pageant, and in this case, where there will be an audience, seating space and stage are required. In this case, the church itself can be used, or an adequate stage in an assembly room may be provided. If a stage is built, it should be provided with adequate lighting facilities and proper equipment for curtain and scene shifting, and the auditorium should have a seating capacity for anticipated audiences.

Another facet of religious education that re-quires special equipment is the audio-visual program. Each departmental room should be equipped so that projected pictures and sound can be used. This will require special lighting arrangements to take care of the equipment and to darken the room during projection. Draperies may be used for darkening the room, and proper ventilation is also very important. Good acoustics, such as a sound-absorbing wall and a ceiling of acoustical tile, will reduce the noise and improve the sound quality. Storage space for audio-visual equipment is also necessary.

Color is important for children, and the Sunday school rooms should have carefully planned color schemes. Here are some suggested color schemes:

1. Window wall, cocoa brown; other walls, light canary yellow; floor, brown asphalt tile; draperies and pictures, in browns, yellows, and accents of orange.

2. Window wall, turquoise; other walls, light yellow; floor, gray asphalt tile; draperies and other wall decorations, gray, yellow, turquoise, and deep blue.

3. Window wall, gray; other walls, ivory; floors, red asphalt tile; draperies and wall decorations, gray, red, and yellow.

4. Window wall, rose; other walls, bone white; floors, green; draperies and wall decorations, rose, green, and yellow.

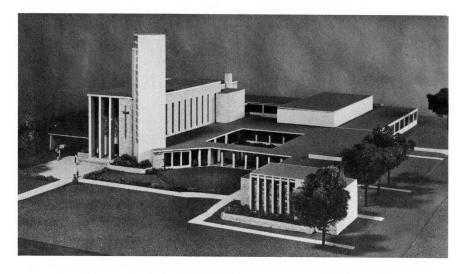

Architect's model for Christ Episcopal Church, Warren, Ohio.

15

Art in the Church

RELIGION and art are closely interwoven. The stories of the Bible and the teachings of the Church are written in the painting and sculpture of the past ages. Most religions have identified their sacraments with art. Religious beliefs have been clothed in pomp and pageantry and they have appealed to the imagination with music, incense, embroidered vestments, and solemn processions. In the Middle Ages, the Christian faith used the power of art and architecture in the Gothic cathedral to teach the most highly spiritualized ideas. On the other hand, the arts hardly had a being outside of the Church. Music, painting, sculpture, architecture, drama, and all the allied arts were the handmaidens of the Church and they depended on the Church for their support.

A study of the art of the ages, at least down to the fifteenth century, necessitates a knowledge of the religious beliefs of the time for a true understanding and appreciation. The artist of past ages did not interpret his individual feelings, but was a trained craftsman who followed carefully the specifications and rules prescribed by the Church. Thus in 787 the Second Council of Nicaea laid down the rule which was binding upon the artists of Christendom for nearly five hundred years: "The substance of religious scenes is not left to the initiative of the artists; it derives from the principles laid down by the Catholic Church and religious tradition. . . . His art alone belongs to the painter, organization and arrangement belong to the clergy."

Thus when the Church of St. Urban of Troyes decided to order a set of tapestries, illustrating the story of St. Valerian and his wife, St. Cecilia, a learned priest wrote the specifications: "There shall be portrayed a place and a tabernacle in the manner of a beautiful room, in which there shall be St. Cecilia, humbly on her knees with her hands joined, praying to God. And beside her shall be Valerian expressing great admiration and watching an angel, which being above their heads should be holding two crowns made of lilies and roses, which he will be placing, the one on the head of St. Cecilia and the other on the head of Valerian, her husband. . . . " The priest who drafted this contract drew his material from the writings of Vincent de Beauvais.

In paintings of the Virgin and Child, not only are the colors, such as the color of the Virgin's robe, prescribed, but each detail in the picture is there because of its meaning rather than for its pure aesthetic value. Thus the interesting fruits in the paintings of Crivelli have symbolic meaning—the cherry in the Christ Child's hand signifying purity. The apple signifies the fall of man, and the pomegranate is an ancient symbol of hope. The bird, so often seen in the hand of the Christ Child, signifies the soul. The lily and the rose, when used as attributes of the Virgin, signify purity, love, and beauty. The enclosed garden seen in the background of many pictures has its source in the Song of Solomon. Each apostle and saint had his own symbols which always accompanied the representation of him.

However, many variations of themes are seen because the clergy ruled the artists with a light hand and they were not even disturbed if secular themes crept in—thus in the illustrations of the Book of Hours the margins are often adorned with scenes from Greek mythology.

However, in the time of the Reformation, the Church began to be more strict in enforcing the rules, and at the Council of Trent in 1563 another edict further deprived the liberty of the artist.

St. Stephen's Episcopal Church, Belvedere, California. The replacement of traditional stained glass and lead by thick glass and reinforced concrete gives a new architectural character to glass—the "stained glass slab." Cummings Studios.

LEFT: One of the two windows in the White Memorial Bay of the National Cathedral, Episcopal, Washington, D. C. Designed and executed by The Willet Stained Glass Co.

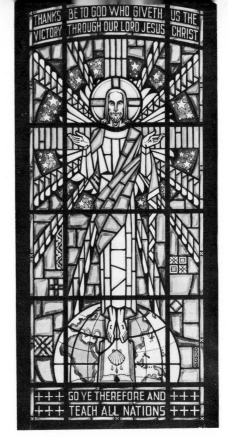

RIGHT: Westminster Presbyterian Church, Detroit, Michigan. The Willet Stained Glass Co.

It not only allowed no work to be placed in the church unless approved by the bishop, but also condemned much of the medieval art.

Thus began the separation of art and religion which was completed by the lack of interest on the part of the clergy and finally by the industrialism of the nineteenth century. The Roman Catholic Church allowed cheap plaster saints, which, though lacking any aesthetic values, violated no laws of the Church. On the other hand, the Protestant Church decoration settled for the pulpit and organ pipes and a few sentimental painted glass windows which ignored both the art of the nineteenth and twentieth centuries and harked back to the past.

It has been a major mistake on the part of the churches to remove the aesthetic value of art, for the greatest art and pure religion are allied. Both beauty and religion have perfection as their goal. Both the religious feeling and intense aesthetic perception take the individual "out of himself" to heights beyond this world. For beauty is something outside of us, the recognition of something greater than the individual. Both beauty and religion attempt to express things unseen and

eternal. Music, poetry, color, and design are new worlds created by the artist. They can and should still be used to help to open the doors of the Kingdom of Heaven. The art of worhip is one of the most beautiful of all the arts, but it needs the aid of all the other arts if it is to be most efficacious.

In recent years since World War II, there has been a growing reapproachment between the Roman Catholic Church and the arts and between Judaism and the arts. They have within the past few decades not only encouraged the best in modern architecture but have commissioned the best artists to do sculpture, painting, and well-designed ceremonial objects. Many Roman Catholic churches have been remodeled and simplified so that renewed emphasis is placed on the altar where the mass is said. There are fewer and better figures of saints, and the beauty of the monastic chapel has been revived in many new Roman Catholic churches.

Judaism has perhaps led all religions in its acceptance of contemporary art to interpret its religion today. In the Jewish church, there are certain required ceremonial objects that can be beautified by the artist. The Ark of stone or wood,

129

Faith-Salem Evangelical and Reformed Church, Jennings, Missouri. The painted-glass mural, depicting the story of Christ, forms the entire front façade of the church. The glass is "Kokomo Seedy" antique glass with the painting fused in, in soft colors of moss green, pink, charcoal gray, white, and, at the Crucifixion panel, a large slab of gold-stained glass. So that the wall of glass could take on the function of exterior decoration as well as help inspire a worshipful mood within the church, color was applied to both the outside and inside surfaces. Thus a reversed view of the mural can be seen from the exterior. The eleven panels were designed by Robert E. Harmon of Emil Frei, Incorporated, which made them. Frederick Dunn & Associates, architects.

131

Window in the Church of the Ascension, Episcopal, Cranston, Rhode Island. Designed and made by Charles J. Connick Associates.

Night effect of window in First Methodist Church, Bridgeport, West Virginia. Designed and made by The Willet Stained Glass Co.

the Tablets of Law, the Candelabrum, the six-pointed Star or Shield of David, and the Eternal Light are necessary appointments of every synagogue.

The Protestant Church is far behind in its recognition of the present-day need of art to assist religion. The Lutherans lead with the most beautiful of the new church buildings. The Episcopalians are still largely concerned with styles of the past, but on the whole the Episcopal churches of the past century were well designed so that they have fewer errors to correct.

One good result in the past few years has been the tendency of Presbyterian, Baptist, and Methodist churches to adopt the formal architectural plan which calls for a chancel and an altar. This not only makes for a better looking church interior, but results in a more formal and more dignified service format.

Indeed much is being done to improve the appearance of the church today, but we are even now neglecting to give recognition to our great painters, sculptors and craftsmen. As a whole, the Church is still satisfied with the factory product

of the religious arts shop instead of calling in the service of a competent artist. We need a deeper conviction regarding the importance of the arts and their contribution to the religious experience.

The major responsibility for art in the church today rests with the clergy. If a minister wishes, he can usually put what he wants in the church, if he can get the support of higher authority, and most of his congregation will accept his judgment. The trouble is that the clergy on the whole are not interested and also that their taste is not trained in art. However, the responsibility for anything relating to the church belongs to the minister.

It is easier to train one clergyman in art appreciation than to try to change the tastes of a whole congregation. To do this, every seminary that prepares men for the ministry should require a course in art appreciation as a part of their training. The course should include art history, which shows the place of art in the church throughout the ages. It should also teach the appreciation of art —what is good and what is bad art—in everyday life, from painting and sculpture down to carpets and office desks. From the theological side, I would have the course include a reading of I Kings, chapters 6 and 7, and all other Bible passages which refer to beauty in the decoration of God's House.

A course in finger painting or clay modeling or sketching would also help. In fact, a seminary class given finger paints and Noah's Ark or Zechariah 1:8 as subject matter might produce some interesting results. First of all they would find that they could get the story across without knowing how to draw. Secondly, they would find that religious art need not depend upon tradition —that there can be new approaches to religious expression.

Naturalism has no place in religious art. Religious art should aim at teaching the ideals and spiritual qualities of religion. The artist may formalize, exaggerate, or stylize in endless techniques. To aim at photographic representation limits the spiritual value of the work of art. In all great religious art of the past, there is a persistent strangeness to the human figures that lifts it above the natural. The conventional representations of Byzantine and Gothic art symbolize the supernatural through abstractions. Such representations of Christ and other biblical figures as painted by Hoffman and his nineteenth-century followers lose the great spiritual qualities of religion.

"O sing unto the Lord a new song"—such is the theme of present-day ecclesiastical art. Religion of the twentieth century is not the same as that of the fifteenth or the nineteenth century—there are new qualities and new interpretations of the age-old truths. Today's religion is modern, that is, it is made for use today. Thus the new religious art must look for new qualities to express. It must take on new forms and a new formal language. The old Renaissance traditions of religious art are lost to many today. For example, the present-day teaching and interpretation of Good Friday is no longer bogged down in the suffering of the Cross as expressed in the hopeless figures of Christ which are brought out in Mexican and other Latin-American countries during Holy

The Judgment Day façade window of St. Gertrude's Church, Franklin Park, Chicago. Designed by Peter Recker and executed by Conrad Schmitt Studios. Belli & Belli, architects.

"Feeding the Multitude"—detail of the Emil Frei painted-glass mural of Faith-Salem Evangelical and Reformed Church, Jennings, Missouri. (See pages 130-131.)

Week. The new figures of Christ on the cross no longer show a suffering, dying, pathetic victim, but a living, regal Christ, alive and serene, looking beyond time to the glory of eternal life.

Religion, to be most effective, must still be communicated by means of symbols. The visible object leads to the invisible, just as the imagery in the Bible is necessary to teach the unseen truth. But even the language of symbolism is simplified today into non-objective forms. Narrative art is out. The artist today looks for the inner truth and beauty. Art is still traditional in content, but not necessarily in form. As the Church seeks to recover its old spontaneity found in such things as the Gregorian chant, so the austerity of modern art seeks a like primitive and spontaneous quality.

New interpretations of art today are also influenced by the use of new materials. The material used for a work of art always puts limitations on what can be expressed. Steel and aluminum crosses do not allow for intricate carving. Instead, the simple cross today is characterized by good proportion and exaggerated size. New materials always give a new beauty—the baptismal font, once the object of elaborate carving and symbolism, has in the modern interpretation become a simple bowl on a pedestal. Yet this simple object is designed with dignity and beauty of proportion that can make it a work of art whether it be constructed of wood and steel, or concrete and brass, instead of marble.

Beauty always varies in proportion to the nature of the thing which is beautiful. The beauty of the sunset is not the same as the beauty of a symphony. The beauty of sculpture is not the same as the beauty of painting or of mosaic. Each is of a different material, and the honest expression, or the limitation, of the material gives it its greatest beauty. There is also the beauty of the craft—the mark of the silversmith's or the ironworker's hammer or the sculptor's chisel. Painting and stained glass depend on color and light for much of their beauty and effectiveness. There is even the beauty of the empty wall—the beauty of silence—which has its place in worship. So in ecclesiastical art today we look for the expression of spiritual power in pure form and in the dignity of simple materials simply used—for the symbolism of pure line, form, and color, rather than ornate details. The best of our contemporary artists are giving us these qualities in present-day religious art, but we must have the inclination and the ability to see and appreciate them.

Sculpture, which is more closely allied to architecture than any other art, has always had a prominent place in the Church. Sculpture was at first a part of the structure, in the form of the carved frieze—in Gothic architecture, figure sculpture was still tied to the structure of the building; and today we use sculpture in the form of bas-relief as well as separate figures. The modern American sculptor seems to be prepared for church work because of his interest in religious subject matter. If the present-day churches do not use the work of American sculptors, it is not for lack of availability. In every section of the country, there are able sculptors. The sculptor may work in stone, marble, wood, metals, terra cotta, or ceramics. Few present-day churches have the funds to erect a carved reredos or pulpit. There are few calls for bronze doors, or carved tympaniums, or figures on portal posts. However, a simply carved doorway, or a single figure, can add much to the appearance of the modern church. There are also crosses, crucifixes, and in the Roman Catholic church, and some Episcopal churches, Stations of the Cross which can all be enhanced by a good sculptor. A beautiful hand-carved cross against a simple background can add more beauty than any other feature in the decoration of the present-day church. There are many architectural uses for sculpture: doorways, window frames, lintels, columns, ceilings, open room spaces, parts of walls, entire walls, or areas in front of walls. The present-day sculptor has extended his art to carved glass and brick, sized slate, and even cut and painted linoleum.

Contemporary church design calls for a new approach to architectural sculpture. New materials such as steel, copper, and aluminum may be called upon to replace stone or wood. Color and light also play an important part in today's church sculpture, but whatever the means of expression, the talents of the sculptor are still needed to give feeling and poetry and to help to suggest architectural space. Architecture separated from art becomes engineering.

The small, architecturally simple church of today is a challenge to the ecclesiastical sculptor. There is no need for a profusion of sacred images as in the past, but a few pieces, or perhaps only one important piece, to aid worship and supply the religious mood and to help effect the emotional satisfaction between man and his environment, are as necessary today as in past ages.

Good church art is possible on a small budget. One focal point should be chosen to supply the

Baltimore Hebrew Congregation, Baltimore, Maryland. Contemporary sculpture for the façade by George Aarons.

religious mood for the whole of a small church. One of the first contemporary churches to be built in this country, St. Mark's Episcopal, in St. Louis, Missouri, illustrates this point. It was built on a close budget utilizing the building construction methods of the twentieth century and relying on proportion and scale for aesthetic effect. The exterior is made distinctive by one large limestone figure of St. Mark, and the interior is given feeling and beauty by a large crucifix of carved wood on a red leather and gold cross. The church was designed by Nagel and Dunn, architects, and the sculpture was the work of Sheila Burlingame.

The recently completed Church of Christ the King, in Dallas, Texas, has an impressive façade dominated by a huge stone carving of Christ the King, with a round window forming the nimbus and surrounded on either side by a choir of carved angels.

A terra-cotta Madonna is the single decoration in the courtyard of the Church of the Rosary at Sun Valley.

The little church of St. Elizabeth, at Burrien, Washington, will have a carved and decorated Tree of Jesse to give distinction to its simple exterior.

A welded bronze sculpture of The Pillar of Fire, by Ibram Lassaw, dominates the exterior of Temple Beth-El, in Springfield, Massachusetts. A single work of sculpture planned with the architect, before building, usually gives more beauty and feeling than many pieces placed after construction. This puts the sculptor in a position where he must come out of the seclusion of his studio and work with the architect rather than working out his own individual expression and hoping that it will find a niche in a church somewhere, some place. In every case, the church sculptor must have humility so that the general mood of the church dominates his individual piece of sculpture.

Although few churches today can afford large mural paintings, there are experienced mural painters in all parts of the country and many who have done church work. Mural painting is the antithesis of easel painting. The approach of the mural artist to his problem is not solved by the enlargement of a picture designed for a frame, but is limited by architectural requirements of space. The mural must be related to the scale and space of the architecture. Naturalistic three-dimensional painting is not adapted to murals and especially not to murals in contemporary buildings. Abstract art is particularly well suited to modern architecture.

Mural painting also must lend itself to the spirit of the architecture. It must conform to the texture of the wall and preserve the flatness and solidity of the wall. Too strong color contrasts will destroy the unity of the wall surface—the mural must also be comparatively flat or it destroys the wall. In a church, the subject matter is not only used as decoration, but it should have some symbolical meaning and connection with the church service. Murals for modern church buildings should be flat, sharp, and distinct in design.

Today, if we use painting in the decoration of the church, it is best to concentrate the painting on the wall of the sanctuary. Several new churches have used murals to decorate their sanctuary walls. Such painting should be considered as decoration, and the subject matter should be simple and symbolical rather than narrative. The design should be relatively flat and conventional so that it "stays on the wall" and the colors should be pure and strong. Religion is not interpreted by pink and baby blue.

The painter should also be employed more often to design and decorate the cross. Crosses may be painted on the sanctuary wall above the altar, or hanging wooden crosses may be painted and decorated. Stations of the Cross may be painted on wood or canvas or directly on a plaster wall. The wall behind the font may be decorated with appropriately painted decoration. Present-day painters are also designing glass, mosaics, enamels, and fabrics for the church. While there is no shortage of painters in America, there seem to be fewer painters than sculptors who are interested in religious art.

Mosaic work, which has long been used in the church, has been having a revival in the last few years. Mosaic is an art wherein small pieces of glass, stone, ceramics, or metals are set in cement. The technique of mosaic makes exactness of draw-

First Baptist Church, Longview, Texas. Figure sculpture by Richard M. Hetrick. Stone sculpture against interesting and imaginative use of brick. Wilson, Morris, & Crain, architects.

is its background, has made radical changes. Indeed, modern architecture no longer forms the proper setting for traditional stained glass. Colored glass windows are, however, still looked upon with favor by the Church, but they should be designed in harmony with the architecture. Stained glass windows provide color, light, and pattern. They should not be a picture but are a portion of the wall made beautiful.

Before a design is made, the artist should know the situation of the building and the natural lighting from the outside. It is necessary, in a successful window, for more light to come from the outside than from the inside. The darker the glass, the less light will come in, but the interior must still be darker or the luminosity is lost. Thus a window placed against an outside brick wall of an adjoining building would lose its luminosity if the interior of the building were too light. Also, if there is too much interior light, the glass will seem harsh and glaring. Deep, rich colored windows should be few and far spaced, so that they will not detract from each other. A stained glass window should be a mosaic of colored light. Its beauty lies in the life and movement of light as

ing difficult and thus a flat, formalized design is the result. The colors of mosaic are usually brilliant and glowing, and this, together with the excessive use of gold, makes them suitable for dimly lighted places such as churches. Mosaics are also effective on exterior walls. There are a few well-known mosaicists, all of whom do religious work, and there are also Italian mosaic companies which execute mosaics after designs by well-known artists.

One of the interesting contemporary developments in the arts especially related to the church is the change that has come about in the design and making of stained glass. Stained glass has been used to temper the light in cathedral windows since the tenth century. The stained glass window was the most effective means of creating atmosphere and adding beauty and color to the Gothic church. The craft of stained and leaded glass window-making has made few changes in the last nine centuries, while architecture, which

One of the fourteen Stations of the Cross in the Church of Our Lady of the Assumption, Ventura, California. Albert Stewart, sculptor.

though the window itself were the source of light.

The colors of a stained glass window change each hour in the day, and there is an ever-changing pattern of tones and hues. The reds and yellows are brighter at midday and the blues are brighter when the light dims. Different colors have different expanding and contracting properties which must be understood by the designer or they will mar his design. Red and blue, for example, radiate violet, and must be used in the right proportion so that the radiation will not interfere with the original concept of the design.

In designing a stained glass window, the artist first makes a small, colored sketch. Then a full-scale drawing or cartoon is made and marked to show the exact sizes and shapes of the glass and to indicate the colors. The glass is then selected and cut to shape, leaving a small margin for the leads. The details of the design are painted in with opaque pigment and the surface fired in the kiln. After that the pieces of the design are assembled with the leads, and H-shaped strips of lead are put on and soldered tight. Stained glass

"Swords into Ploughshares," by Moissaye Marans, designed for The Community Church of New York, New York City.

is set in stone, steel, or wood frames which, when properly spaced, do not mar but enhance the design.

Modern techniques fuse crushed bits of glass to the larger surface of glass and get an effect of sparkling and shifting luminosity. Thick chips of glass are often embedded in cement in a mosaic effect. Leadings are now designed in sculptural forms which show in the daylight of the exterior and are outlined against the colored glass pattern at night.

Modern stained glass often sustitutes stone or concrete for leads. In modern stained glass, an indefinite number of color changes is possible by means of staining, plating, aciding, or embossing. Two or more layers of glass can be superimposed within one leaded area. Acid and painting and a batik technique can be used. New effects are also gained by a contrast of plain clear glass and glass that has bubbles. This contrast in glass texture

"Virgin and Child," in brown terra cotta, by Henry Rox.

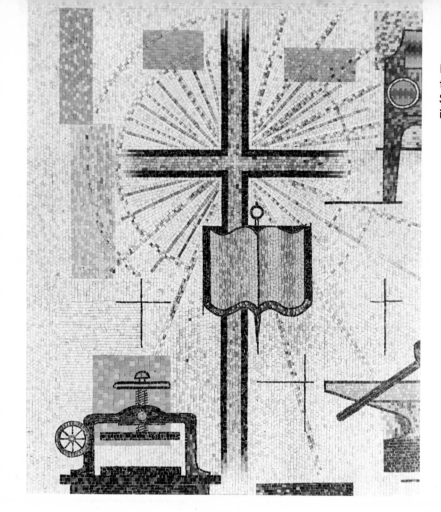

Detail of the mosaic wall from the entrance to Don Bosco Technical High School, Roman Catholic, San Gabriel, California, by Joseph Young.

also allows for different effects of light. Stained glass techniques have also been applied to such modern materials as plate glass and glass block. All these new methods give a greater sense of transparency, translucency, and opacity. The designs of much modern stained glass are simple, so that costs of workmanship are cut down. Patterns are simplified to harmonize with modern simplicity in architecture. An interesting example is the abstract design of glass by Robert Stowers for St. George's Episcopal Church, Durham, New Hampshire. The abstract pattern of blue, white, yellow, red, and purple glass is similar to that of the fieldstone in the construction of the church building. Steel and aluminum allow whole walls to be constructed of glass and several colors of rectangular panes of glass of different sizes are used without any design at all, and when planned by a designer who understands light and glass, these simple windows speak a language similar to that of the old stained glass.

Stained glass has been made in America since the middle of the nineteenth century. Unfortunately, much of the American-made glass was pictorial, or of inferior workmanship, so that it is not desirable today. A complete history of stained glass in America and names of the makers is written by Harold W. Rambusch and Henry Lee Willet and is found in the *Encyclopedia Americana,* 1948 Edition. Today studios, designers, and workmen in stained glass are located in almost every part of America.

Artists in metalwork are needed to design and execute iron, bronze, and aluminum gates, grilles, and communion rails. Today there is also sculpture of steel, copper, and aluminum. Much beautiful metalwork is to be seen in the churches in large American cities, and interesting metalwork is still being designed and used in churches. The well-known artists working in this medium are not as plentiful as the painters and sculptors. The Jewish synagogue uses more metalwork than other churches and for this reason Jewish artists have done the best-known metalwork today.

Temple Emanuel, Beverly Hills, California. Italian glass mosiac mural in the entranceway depicts the three main functions of the contemporary temple—study, prayer, and assembly. Over eighty colors, together with gold, were used. The mosaic is the work of Joseph Young. The temple, designed by Sidney Eisenshtat, also features the work of Bernard Rosenthal. Sculpture and enamels by Arthur and Jean Ames.

Reliquary (or Treasure Case) in bronze and enamel. Height one foot, eight inches. Designed for Holy Cross Church, St. Louis, Missouri, by Wilhelm Wagner.

Enamelwork on metal is another art medium used in the decoration of church articles such as crosses, candlesticks, and church vessels, as well as decoration for altar fronts, wall plaques, and Stations of the Cross. One of the altar fronts in St. Mark's, Venice, is of Byzantine enamel, and such articles as reliquary boxes and crosses are made of French champlevé enamel. Enamel work is really a jeweler's art. The design is sketched on a metal base, usually copper. Then the design is eaten out with acid, and an engraver's tool is used to make a surface that the enamel will cling to. The colored glass is ground to powder and mixed with a binder, painted on the surface, and then baked on. When the baking is done, the surface is ground and then repainted and refired. This repeated firing and painting give a brilliant and lustrous color and make the surface smooth and hard as stone. In old Persian and Byzantine enamels, thin wire lines are used to divide the colors, and in the best work today this same technique is followed.

All these allied arts are needed for church decoration. It is in the accessories of worship that a church takes on individual character. Just one beautiful object in a church—the altar, or the cross, or one stained glass window—can set the tone for the whole building. It is to be hoped that the thousands of Americans visiting Chartres and Notre Dame in Paris will return with a desire to have more beauty in their parish church.

Indeed, if present-day church architecture is to present a spiritual as well as a functional concept, the architect must accept the help of color, mosaic, stained glass, sculpture, and mural painting, as well as the other allied arts. Architecture stripped to the bone becomes engineering. It must be humanized with color. The architect must realize this and plan for the use of color through the arts or he runs the risk of having his architecture draped and carpeted and cushioned by decorators who may destroy the foundations of his architectural plan.

Enamel pyx by Kenneth Francis Bates. The Cleveland Museum of Art, Gift of The Cleveland Art Association.

Bibliography

Addleshaw, G. W. O., and Etchells, F., *The Architectural Setting of Anglican Worship*. London, Faber and Faber, 1948.

Cox, John Charles, *Pulpits, Lecterns, Organs*. London, Oxford University Press, 1915.

de Farcy, Louis, *La Broiderie du XIe Siècle*. Paris, E. Leroux, 1890.

Dewey, John, *Art as Experience*. New York, G. P. Putnam's Sons, 1934.

Drummond, Andrew Londale, *Church Architecture of Protestantism*. Edinburgh, T. and T. Clark, 1934.

Green, E. Tyrell, *Baptismal Fonts*. London, Society for Promoting Christian Knowledge, 1928.

Hamlin, Talbot, ed., *Forms and Functions of Twentieth Century Architecture*, 4 vols. New York, Columbia University Press, 1952.

Joint Commission on Architecture and the Allied Arts, *Architecture and the Church*. Greenwich, Conn., Seabury Press, 1952.

Rock, Daniel, *The Church of Our Fathers as Seen in St. Osmund's Rite for the Cathedral of Salisbury*, 4 vols. London, John Murray, 1905.

Santayana, George, *The Sense of Beauty*. New York, Charles Scribner's Sons, 1938.

Victoria and Albert Museum, *Textile Fabrics: a Descriptive Catalogue of the Collection of Church Vestments*. South Kensington, 1870.

von Falke, Otto, *Decorative Silks*. New York, William Helburn, Inc., 1922.

Photograph Acknowledgments

Ankers Photographers, 104
Charles Baptie, top 18, 73
Frank H. Bauer, 114
Cleveland Museum of Art, bottom 142
Walter S. Craig, 42
Bill Engdahl, Hedrich-Blessing, 26
"Frashers" Fotos, bottom 138
Don Garber Photography, left 97
Alexandre Georges, 72
Edward H. Goldberger, 117, 118
Samuel H. Gottscho, 36
A. Hansen Studio, top 84, bottom 84, bottom 85, 91, 93, top 94, 98, 99
Walt Hawver, Daily News, Burlington, Vt., top 27
Hedrich-Blessing, 15, 53
Bill Hedrich, Hedrich-Blessing, 77, 123
Hube Henry, Hedrich-Blessing, 61, 64
Art Hupy, 37, 75
George Lindsay, 54
James Ellery Marble, 71
Martin's Studio, 115
Dewey G. Mears, 16
Joseph W. Molitor, 35
Moulin Studios, 128
I. Mull Photography, 20, 76
Museum of Modern Art, New York, 81
Budd Nease, 51
Marc Neuhof, 49
Paget, 18, 24, bottom 27, 28
Reynolds Photography, Inc., 46, 47
Dale Rooks, 65, 110, 116
Walter Rosenblum, 82
George Miles Ryan Studios, Inc., 40
F. W. Seiders, top 138
David Shore, 124
Julius Shulman, 141
Roger Sturtevant, 2
Timber Structures, Inc., 44